SECRET WIRRAL

Les Jones

AMBERLEY

First published 2020

Amberley Publishing
The Hill, Stroud
Gloucestershire, GL5 4EP

www.amberley-books.com

Copyright © Les Jones, 2020

The right of Les Jones to be identified as the Author
of this work has been asserted in accordance with
the Copyrights, Designs and Patents Act 1988.

ISBN 978 1 4456 5341 9 (print)
ISBN 978 1 4456 5342 6 (ebook)

British Library Cataloguing in Publication Data.
A catalogue record for this book is available from the
British Library.

Origination by Amberley Publishing.
Printed in Great Britain.

Contents

Introduction   4

1   Tales from the Tower   5

2   It Happened Here   16

3   Village Secrets   23

4   Smugglers and Wreckers   55

5   The Peoples Garden   64

6   The Leisure Peninsula   71

Introduction

Much has been written about Wirral over the years: the stories of the model village at Port Sunlight, the mighty shipyards of Cammell Lairds and the ancient priory in Birkenhead are all well known. This book seeks to highlight some of the lesser-known facts about our beautiful peninsula, with accounts of hidden caves, secret war factories, forgotten cinemas and a host of interesting characters who have all played a part in the area's varied history. Interspersed within the text are numerous 'Did You Know?' boxes with quirky facts about Wirral and its more eccentric inhabitants.

We begin on a nondescript grassy bank in New Brighton. It is not much to look at nowadays, but was once home to probably the greatest entertainment complex in Britain, the Alton Towers of its day, crowned by the tallest structure in the country. The Tower Grounds still evoke the fondest of memories from locals and visitors old enough to remember them in their heyday in the 1950s, before the pull of foreign climes and the lure of television caused visitor numbers to decline, leading to its ultimate demise, hastened by a devastating fire in 1969.

The popularity of Wirral to the entertainment industry is covered in Chapter 2, with a tremendous variety of locations and an impressive cast of entertainers who have plied their art on our peninsula. From the prosaic backdrops of Wallasey Docks and the Mersey Tunnel, we are transported in our imaginations to the Olympic Games in 1920s France, or the gangland of Birmingham just after the First World War. There follows a short but informative tour of some of the diverse villages that give Wirral its unique character, from the once-rural villages swallowed up by the urban sprawl of Birkenhead and Wallasey, to the bucolic mid-Wirral villages and the mysterious Shotwick, tucked away to the south. All have an interesting and varied story to tell. We then meet a cast of smugglers and ne'er-do-wells who went about their illicit business on the wild and savage coasts that surround the peninsula, stories of hidden booty and the constant need to keep one step ahead of the customs men, and tales of supernatural beings conjured up by the inventive smugglers to keep the curious away from the sites of their nefarious nocturnal doings.

We then take a more sedate stroll around Birkenhead's famous park, showing how a few talented and forward-thinking men created this magnificent space in a rapidly expanding town, showcasing its many lesser-known attractions such as the lodges at each entrance, each with its own unique architecture. Finally, indulging in pure nostalgia, we trace the fascinating development of sport and entertainment on Wirral, from the early cinemas and earlier music halls to the many sports enjoyed throughout the peninsula. Golf plays a major role in attracting tourism to the area, but it is a lesser-known fact that horse racing was once the main attraction. Both are discussed in this final chapter, together with other sports popular on Wirral, leading it to be rightly known as 'the Leisure Peninsula'.

I hope those of you who know Wirral well will find something new here, and those who are looking to visit will be encouraged to seek out some more of the secrets of Wirral.

1. Tales from the Tower – New Brighton Tower Grounds, the Original Alton Towers

Little evidence remains of the vast 35-acre leisure complex known as the New Brighton Tower Grounds. A steep grassy ridge leads up to a small estate of houses called River View Park whose streets gently evoke echoes of its former glory, Lakeside Court, Tower Court and Rakersfield Road.

Wealthy shipowner Robert Houston had a big idea in the late 1890s, to build a leisure complex in the burgeoning resort of New Brighton to rival nearby Blackpool. He set up the Tower Estate Syndicate Limited and sold shares to raise sufficient capital to bring his project to fruition. A large tract of land adjacent to the River Mersey belonging to the Molyneux family was bought for £300,000. It consisted of a large property called Rock Point House and its estate, providing the space required for the development to begin.

The site of the old Tower Grounds, 2019.

Tower and Lake, New Brighton

New Brighton Tower and the lake, 1904.

Originally called The Plantation, the grounds were developed into one of the largest tourist attractions in the United Kingdom, its famous tower fully 621 feet above sea level and dwarfing its nearest rival at Blackpool. Built between 1897 and 1900 by Maxwell and Tuke who also designed Blackpool Tower and Southport Winter Gardens, the structure was made of steel rather than iron, costing £120,000 – a colossal sum at the time. A 1s (5p) entrance fee bought a ride in one of the four lifts up to the observation tower, the so-called Eyrie, where peerless views of the Liverpool Docks and the Wirral Peninsula could be experienced. These extended to the Isle of Man and Llandudno on a clear day. Despite its world-beating dimensions, however, the tower proved to be an expensive white elephant and, partly due to a lack of maintenance to the structure during the First World War, it was dismantled between 1919 and 1921.

DID YOU KNOW?
In the 1950s the Tower Ballroom attracted some of the biggest dance band leaders, such as Joe Loss and Victor Sylvester. Whenever the band took a break all the top dancers would leave the dancefloor and the beginners came on, dancing to recorded music. All the better dancers refused to dance to mere records as they rather sniffily felt that it was not 'proper music' and would not catch on.

Below the Tower was an equally grandiose red-brick ballroom, which regularly attracted over 1,000 couples, dancing the night away in luxuriant surroundings on a specially sprung dancefloor, surrounded by painted panels of civic insignia of nearby Lancashire and Cheshire towns. A further 500 could be accommodated around the perimeter. Other draws over the years included the Tower Theatre where a guinea bought an evening's entertainment with such luminaries as Harry Lauder, Vesta Tilley and Edward Elgar. To mark the end of the First World War a victory concert was held with a full choir conducted by Stainton de B. Taylor who lived in the nearby Roundhouse. Such highbrow entertainment diminished over the years with downmarket exhibitions such as Al (Scarface) Capone's $20,000 bulletproof gangster car and, latterly, wrestling becoming the main attraction.

A popular museum was created in the 1920s where tourists could while away an hour or so surveying colourful tableaux of native Canadian Indians and trappers, worthies such as Earl Kitchener, Baden-Powell and Gordon of Khartoum, and a large collection of Japanese artefacts including guitars, clogs, wooden pillows and other random paraphernalia.

One of the fondest memories many have of the tower, however, was the waxworks. Popular exhibits included models of George V, Robbie Burns, the Archbishop of Canterbury, Adolf Hitler and Gandhi – strange bedfellows indeed. While all this was most educational, what most people turned up to see was the infamous Chamber of Horrors where such delights as the gibbet, the scolds bridle, branding, the rack and, a particular

New Brighton Tower Ballroom, 1920.

Gondolas on the lake *c.* 1900.

The top of the water chute, *c.* 1910.

The scenic railway, 1922.

favourite, pressing to death, could be gawped at by the great unwashed. The horrors concluded with a group of notorious characters including John Jackson, the Strangeways murderer; William Fish, the Blackburn murderer; and, curiously, David Davies, the Dartmoor Shepherd?!

Further delights awaited the day trippers and tourists outside where proprietors vied for custom with countless diversions. In the early days genuine Venetian gondoliers in authentic gondolas (minus the cornetto) touted for business on a large ornamental lake, located to the south of Egerton Street where a five-a-side pitch now stands. Two artificial lakes were created to the east and west, with a popular 130-foot water chute ride for the more adventurous leading in from the south-west. To the north of the lake stood a large Japanese café, the grandest of the eating establishments on the site, with other fare available at the Parisian Tea Gardens where customers could relax and enjoy a Pierrot show. There was an Algerian café and for fine dining there was the Rock Point Castle restaurant at the top of an old quarry, converted from the original Rock Point House. The quarry itself was brought into use with a huge rockery planted with ferns and creepers, an ornamental fountain and even a seal pond. This sheltered area proved popular on a hot summer day as somewhere to cool off and relax.

Nearby stood another of the major draws: a Himalayan switchback railway, which proved a most popular amusement. It was later replaced by a more sedate scenic railway. After sampling these delights, visitors could take a short stroll over to the menagerie and lion house where two once proud lions – Pasha and Prince – were forced to endure the

NB 27 · NEW BRIGHTON. GENERAL VIEW FROM TOP OF THE TOWER

View from the top of the Tower Building, 1957.

constant attention of thousands of people each day. Worse was to follow when a couple of old tramcar bodies were pressed into service as animal houses where bedraggled monkeys and other non-domestic fauna were displayed for the edification of the crowd. Luckily all this was swept away when proprietors brought in more rides and amusements to occupy the tourists. Further down towards the promenade was an American skating rink on an elevated platform and one of New Brighton's five bandstands where a military band played at frequent intervals throughout the day.

The 1930s brought a raft of new attractions to the Tower Grounds. Among the newcomers were the ghost train, motor dodgems, the Skid ride 'for those wanting thrills', the Caterpillar ('thrills without spills') and the Ben Hur ride ('fun and exciting'), all of which proved most popular. Meanwhile the lake had lost its gondolas and the gondoliers had returned to Venice. Both of the artificial lakes were removed along with the water chute and rowing boats and canoes were introduced – self-propulsion was now the order of the day.

One of the longer-lasting rides that endured into the 1960s was the Figure of Eight switchback, which many residents and visitors will remember. Positioned adjacent to Tower Promenade, it offered a fine view of the Mersey for those braver souls not thundering around the rickety structure with their eyes closed. It was a genuinely scary experience, enhanced no doubt by the thought that the whole edifice felt as if it could tumble down onto the prom at any given moment. The loud clack-clack-clack of the ratchet as it raised the cars to the top of the roller coaster could be heard all over

GENERAL VIEW FROM TOWER, NEW BRIGHTON.

View of the Tower Grounds showing the Figure of Eight and pier.

the grounds throughout the day and into the evening. One experience strictly for the professional daredevil was the Wall of Death, definitely not for the have-a-go hero looking to impress his latest squeeze. Other ways to exhibit alpha-male behaviour were available at the rifle range and the coconut shy.

The children were not ignored either, as plenty of attractions were geared up for their amusement. The Caterpillar was a sedate enough circular affair where a large canopy enveloped the passengers at intervals throughout the three-minute ride. Most visitors will remember the rides designed for the younger element as these same people will now all be in their sixties and seventies. The smaller stalls included one that this author particularly remembers whereby a ping-pong ball was rolled down a chute in an effort to drop it into the open mouth of a clown at the bottom, the achievement of which elicited a sense of enormous pride and the reward of a china clay dog, a bow and arrow, or a real goldfish in a plastic bag. Less esoteric pleasures were to be had on the immensely popular children's train operated by Tommy Mann, which slowly chugged its way around a short section alongside the promenade before turning inland through a tunnel towards the quarry and back to the start. Simple pleasures.

As health and safety was not such an all-encompassing facet of day-to-day life in those far-off times, no one thought it inappropriate to haul small children into a tiny metal cage with a small chain slung across as a perfunctory safety measure, before lifting them 50 feet into the air towards the side of the Tower Building on one of the later attractions to grace the Tower Grounds. The chairlift to the top and back again was an exhilarating experience for many and gave another great view of the funfair and the Mersey, but in

UNCLE TOMMY'S SUPER MINIATURE RAILWAY,   TOWER PROMENADE,   NEW BRIGHTON.

Tommy Mann's miniature railway, *c.* 1954.

A view of the chairlift in 1948.

retrospect it is a miracle that more people did not meet their Maker by slipping out of the flimsy gondolas.

All the merriment outlined above was predominantly focussed on the summer season but the wise heads who created these attractions knew that they needed something to appeal to the public during the leaner winter months. This was the main reason for the creation of the New Brighton Athletic Ground, which was constructed at the top of the site to the south of the tower. As with most things pertaining to the Tower Grounds, the stadium was built on a grand scale with an outer cycle track, an inner running track and a central arena with a capacity of a staggering 100,000. From the start the dominant sport taking place was football, the first team to play here being New Brighton Tower FC. Unfortunately, they only managed three seasons in the Lancashire League, although they were League champions in their first season. Very poor attendances (average gate: 1,000) led to their demise, with Doncaster Rovers taking their place in 1901. New Brighton FC lasted rather longer, gaining a place in the Third Division (North) in 1921 until they too were voted out, with Workington Town replacing them. They only played at the Tower Ground from 1946 when they moved from their Rake Lane ground after war damage, hence the nickname of the Rakers. In 1923 the World Cycling Championships were held here, and speedway was very popular in the 1930s. It was also used over the years for many large events, from gatherings of scouts to military tattoos. The stadium, however, mirrored the decline of the Tower Grounds and by the 1960s stock car racing was the main draw, despite the fact that planning permission had never actually been granted. The inevitable decline after the fire in 1969 culminated in the ground being given over to housing.

Boy Scouts parade at the Athletic Ground, September 1909.

Poster advertising the Beatles at the Tower Theatre, 1962.

The Tower Grounds enjoyed their most popular times in the 1950s and early 1960s, by which time cheap foreign holidays and the promise of guaranteed sunshine were reducing the numbers coming to New Brighton and most other UK resorts. One of the highlights of this decade, however, was the frequent appearances of the Beatles at the Tower Ballroom. Their first concert was on 10 November 1961 when they topped the bill of Operation Big Beat, an event organised by Sam Leach which also featured Gerry and the Pacemakers and Rory Storm and the Hurricanes. They were to appear on no fewer than twenty-seven occasions, with their final concert being on 14 June 1963. They had top billing on all but one of their performances, playing second fiddle on 12 October 1962 to none other than Little Richard.

The Tower Grounds from Marine Promenade, 1950.

The death knell, however, finally came in 1969 when the Tower Ballroom was engulfed in a massive blaze, which left it a burnt-out shell. No positive cause was ever established for the fire, but it signalled the terminal decline of a magnificent public space, much-loved by millions of people, tourists and residents alike. There has been a welcome renaissance of New Brighton over recent years with talk of building another Tower funded by the National Lottery, although this particular idea has come to nought. All that remains of the Tower Grounds is a bare grassy knoll. Stand here for a while and the screeches and cries of thousands of happy visitors may be briefly caught in the imagination before drifting off in the evening breeze.

DID YOU KNOW?
In 1909 a mother and her son went up to the top of the tower. They had rather more time than they bargained for to enjoy the view, however, as they missed the last lift down and somehow missed the final inspection, forcing them to stay up there all night. They were eventually rescued at 10 a.m. the next morning, apparently none the worse for their nocturnal adventure.

2. It Happened Here – Wirral Goes to the Movies

The Wirral Peninsula contains rolling hills, industrial streetscapes, quiet villages, noisy towns, and wide-open vistas across to Wales. It can be peaceful, and it can be raucous, but it is never dull. This diversity has provided film makers and television producers with a broad canvas on which to project many of their cinematic concepts. Whether it is recreating the 1924 Olympic Stadium or a Harry Potter chase, a backdrop to the felonious activities of 1920s gangsters or as the surreal background in a pop video, Wirral continues to attract some of the greatest names in Hollywood to our region.

Probably the most well-known film to be shot here was *Chariots of Fire* (1981), the story of two rival athletes, Eric Liddell, a devout Scottish Christian, and Harold Abrahams, an English Jew, and their differing religious convictions. Producer David Putnam needed to recreate the Stade Colombes in Paris during the 1924 Olympic Games and decided upon the Bebington Oval Sports Centre, due predominantly to its 1920s-style entrance. Many of the major scenes in the film were shot here. The scenes where Liddell and Abrahams leave for Paris on the boat train were shot inside the Woodside Ferry Terminus and the

The main entrance to Bebington Oval Sports Centre.

Woodside Ferry Terminal Building.

walkway down to the ferry. Probably the most famous scene from the film, however, shows the athletes running in slow motion along the beach to the strains of Vangelis' unforgettable theme tune; this was all shot at New Brighton.

Let Him Have It (1991) was the story of two small-time would-be burglars called Christopher Craig and Derek Bentley. Craig shot a policeman who was attempting to arrest them, but it was Bentley who went to the gallows for the crime, Craig escaped this fate because of his age. The crime was perpetrated in Croydon, but director Peter Medak decided to use New Brighton for some of the scenes. A poorly lit Victoria Road was used as a backdrop for atmospheric scenes with Bentley during his time as a road sweeper for the council. Some minor scenes were also shot in New Brighton for *Florence Foster Jenkins* (2016), a film starring Hugh Grant and Meryl Streep whose appearance in the area during filming created quite a stir. Some scenes were also filmed in Hoylake.

Nick Murphy, the director of the low-budget thriller *Blood* (2012) hailed from West Kirby and went to school in Hoylake, so it was only natural that as part of the plot he would have one of the protagonists bury a body on Hilbre Island. Some minor shots were also filmed in Seacombe. Seacombe also played host to a few scenes from *The Reckoning* (1970), namely Wheatland Lane, the famous (to Wallaseyans) Hector Jackson's scrapyard, and in Daisy Grove, which has subsequently been pulled down. The main actor, Nicol Williamson, also goes for a stroll in the area and the backdrops include the Four Bridges and the Dock Road in Birkenhead, and King Street petrol station in Wallasey. The docks

Flour mills on the Dock Road, Wallasey.

were also briefly seen in the Samuel L Jackson vehicle *51st State* (2001), namely the former flour mills on the Dock Road that have now been converted into luxury apartments.

Probably the most popular location of all, however, is the Queensway Road Tunnel, which has provided the backdrop for scenes from *The Fast and the Furious 6* (2013), *Jack Ryan: Shadow Recruit* (2014) and most famously for a hair-raising chase through the muggle-filled tunnel between Harry Potter and Hagrid in a flying motorbike and sidecar, defying the unwelcome attentions of the hideous Death Eaters. Film makers still utilise the Wirral Peninsula, with these connections being set to continue with the 2019 release of the biopic *Tolkein*, which has used the Ellesmere Port Boat Museum and Port Sunlight model village as locations.

> DID YOU KNOW?
> Everyone who turned up at Bebington Oval in dark clothing as extras for the film *Chariots of Fire* was entered into a prize draw to win a brand-new car.

All of the films mentioned thus far have contained one or two scenes based on Wirral, but the final film summarised here was shot almost entirely in the area and has gone down as a classic – not so much for the plot, which is fairly mundane, but for the

The steps featured in *The Magnet*.

evocative and nostalgic scenes shot in New Brighton, which have become social history in their own right. I refer, of course, to *The Magnet* (1950), an Ealing comedy shot in black and white but none the worse for that. The plot surrounds a small boy played by James Fox (here billed as William Fox) who becomes an accidental hero when he steals a magnet. The story is somewhat irrelevant to most local viewers; it is the superb background scenery that captures the attention and is outlined here scene by scene. After a few scenes shot in Ealing with such stalwarts as Sam Kydd and James Robertson Justice, the action moves to the New Brighton Pier and a longer shot taken from the sands nearby. Both scenes evoke strong memories for many, especially as the pier has been demolished. We move on to a scene taken further along the sands with a good view of Fort Perch Rock in the background, which is fortunately extant. We then see our hero coming off the beach via a flight of steps, which are still there but have been blocked off to the public. Master Fox then descends another flight of steps, which were retained when the new Floral Pavilion was built. Probably the most redolent scenes follow when Fox is seen at the corner of the fabulous art deco Palace Amusement Park before an even better scene inside that will surely conjure up many memories from anyone who has ever whiled away a few hours in this marvellous space. More scenes follow in the alleys around Hope Street and Duke Street, and a number of scenes taken inside the equally art deco New Brighton bathing pool before we see shots taken from the hills in Harrison Park, which has changed little over the years. Several local roads are captured in the sequence where the boy is running away from the police. He runs from Sea Road around

Ellesmere Port Boat Museum.

the corner into Grove Road and up to Kirkway and Mount Pleasant Road. He is visibly out of puff when he reaches home, which is not surprising as it is a house in Ealing. Some of the final scenes show the boy getting into a Jacobs delivery van, which travels along Seabank Road and Duke Street before entering the Birkenhead Tunnel. The film ends with shots taken in Liverpool.

Television producers have not ignored Wirral either, with many fine productions being filmed on the peninsula. BBC's *Peaky Blinders* has used Port Sunlight in many atmospheric shots, although the series is based in Birmingham. Seacombe Ferry has also featured in the series. Ex Member of Parliament Michael Portillo has visited Wirral many times in his various tv shows. The ever-popular *Great Railway Journeys* has seen him visit Birkenhead Park and Port Sunlight and in an earlier show he became a single parent attempting to live on £80 a week while keeping down two jobs. The series was filmed in a house in Evelyn Road in Wallasey.

The Antiques Roadshow has come from Port Sunlight and its spin-off *Antiques Road Trip* has been to Hoylake and Wallasey. The latter town was also the venue for an episode of *Changing Rooms* when the team set about ruining a house in Marlowe Road. *Grand Designs* spent a few months watching a wooden packing crate masquerading as a house being built on Grange Road in West Kirby. An episode of *Foyles War* with Michael Kitchen was also shot in West Kirby (Brookfield Gardens), while nearby Hoylake played host to episodes of *Mary Queen of Shops* and Peter Kays *Car Share*, which had scenes on Hoylake front. Nearby Meols was the location for the mother's house in the comedy *Watching* with Lisa Tarbuck and Paul Bown. The popular *Who Do You Think You Are?* has featured Paul Hollywood with scenes in New Brighton and Vic Reeves bidding farewell

Evelyn Road, Wallasey, home to Michael Portillo.

to a relative in Seacombe Ferry. *The House Detectives* with Dan Cruikshank and Juliet Morris investigated the history of Church Farm in Bidston Village in 1990. Many other TV shows have featured Wirral and it is always good to recognise even a fleeting glimpse of somewhere familiar.

One final mention should be made, not of a film or tv show but a pop promotional video. 'Wonderful Life', a melancholy little ditty by Black, uses Kings Parade in New Brighton as the backdrop for a typically surreal promo, with the art deco public conveniences getting themselves a starring role. All rather strange. Incidentally, this same stretch of coast was used in a Channel 4 ident from 2017 featuring a group of wheelchair racers and the now familiar giant metal figure made up from the Channel 4 logo.

DID YOU KNOW?
James Fox gave up acting soon after *The Magnet* and got a job in a bank. When he was offered a part in the hit film *The Loneliness of the Long-Distance Runner* his father tried to dissuade him from renewing his acting career as he thought banking was a far more respectable calling. How times change.

Art deco at Kings Parade, New Brighton.

3. Village Secrets – Tales from Nine Settlements of Wirral

There is no such thing as an average Wirral village. The archetypal chocolate box village exists of course, with church, pub and wisteria-draped cottages, the majority of which formed organically over centuries, generally within the central and southern parts of the peninsula. Then there are the man-made villages. Bromborough Pool village was the first, but by far the most famous is Port Sunlight, near Bebington, created by Lord Leverhulme out of a virtual swamp on the banks of the Mersey to house his soap factory and his workers. Finally, there are the villages that have been absorbed into the conurbations of Wallasey and Birkenhead. Each has its history, but space does not allow a discussion of them all. The nine villages chosen, however, encompass the variety existing within the peninsula and convey some of the more unusual facts about these areas.

Shotwick Village

To visit Shotwick is to go back in time, so untouched is this tiny land-locked village by the twenty-first century. The village ends in a cul-de-sac, and it has no pub, no school, no shops. What it does possess is a timeless, peaceful atmosphere, untroubled by the modern world. It was not always so. Before the canalisation of the Dee in 1735 took the river miles away from Shotwick and created the vast expanse of land now known as Sealand, the village was the major crossing point from England to Wales in this area, a ford ran from the side of the church all the way to Flint Castle on the Welsh side. This ford was used on several occasions to invade Wales, initially by Henry III in 1245 and then by his son Edward I in 1278 and again in 1284, when he set about building most of the great castles on the north Wales coast that still impress today. The waters of the Dee lapped against the church wall at this time and there is still an iron securing ring there to prove it. So important was the ford that Shotwick Castle was built to protect its northern flank from invading Welshmen, its southern flank being protected by a fortified manor house. The incumbents of the church were known as Chaplains of the Ford; indeed, the church is dedicated to St Michael, patron saint of soldiers. As with most medieval churches, the south porch became central to many of the village activities. Markets were held there, schooling for the small local community, and general parochial business. Evidence of its use during obligatory archery practice at the nearby butts is revealed by the deep scratch marks in the porch wall, made by the locals sharpening the tips of their arrows. The body of the church is twelfth century but the tower dates from the sixteenth. There is much to see inside: box pews and a rare three-decker pulpit, a thirteenth-century font and plenty besides. Unfortunately, it did not completely escape the attentions of the Victorian restorers, but much original fabric has been retained. The village pub, the Greyhound, closed over 100 years ago in 1915, mainly due to the rowdiness of the Irish workers who came over from the dry Welsh side on the Sabbath to imbibe rather too freely as far as the locals were concerned.

St Michael's Church at Shotwick, looking west.

St Michael's Church at Shotwick, showing arrow marks in the south porch.

Oxton Village

The settlement of Oxton Village predates Birkenhead, the town that was eventually to subsume it, by at least 1,000 years. Its antiquity may be greater, however, as a hoard of coins dating from the reigns of Antonius (AD 138–161) and Victorinus (AD 268–271) were discovered in 1854 at the Arno quarry nearby. It lies on a high sandstone ridge that originally boasted fine elevated views across the Mersey, which would eventually attract the merchants of Liverpool to leave their grimy, polluted city and move to leafy Wirral, building many of the fine Victorian villas still with us today.

The greatest date in the history of Oxton must surely be in 1521 when the land was conveyed to George Talbot, the 4th Earl of Shrewsbury. The land was of poor agricultural quality and the whole area became a wasteland. Writing in 1819, Ormerod called Oxton 'mean and small, composed of wretched straggling huts amongst impassable roads'. Little had changed by the time William Mortimer described the area as 'dreary and desolate, presenting a scene of extreme misery and destitution'. This dramatically changed with the expansion of Liverpool as a mercantile and commercial centre when cotton brokers and shipowners bought leases on land owned by the 15th, 16th and 17th Earls of Shrewsbury. The leaseholders set about building suitably grand villas in large grounds surrounded and secluded by substantial sandstone walls, naming many of the subsequent roads rather sycophantically after the Talbots and their numerous titles. We thus have not only Shrewsbury Road and Talbot Roads, but Alton Road (named after the earl's country seat in Staffordshire), Waterford Road (the earl was also Earl of Waterford), Ingestre Road (they were also at one time Viscounts of Ingestre in Staffordshire), Chetwynd Road (another of their titles), Grafton Street (the 19th Earl was Lord of Grafton), Wexford Road

Oxton Village, *c.* 1905.

Rose Mount, Oxton, 1925.

(home county of the 16th Earl's wife), Beresford Road (maiden name of the 18th Earl's wife), and Brancote Road (a model farm owned by the 18th Earl). One of the grandest villas was Oxton Hall, not to be confused with the nearby Old Oxton Hall, which was one of the few substantial houses built before the nineteenth century. Smaller terraces were also constructed to house many of the white-collar workers escaping the grimy city. A small commercial centre was built at the heart of the village in Rose Mount and several pubs, two of which remain as originally built – The Shrewsbury Arms and The Queens.

This change from rural hamlet to Victorian commuter settlement created a village that has remained surprisingly unchanged to this day. There has been some unsympathetic infill when some of the older houses fell into dereliction or were bombed during the war, but by and large the character remains, due in part to the leasehold system where the landowner retained control of building quality and scope, rather like a mini Mayfair where the Duke of Westminster retains similar control over his estates. After becoming a civil parish in 1866 it became part of Birkenhead in 1898 and a conservation area in 1979.

DID YOU KNOW?
The Secret Gardens of Oxton is an annual charity event when around twenty beautiful private gardens are opened up to for the delectation of the public, allowing a unique opportunity to view domestic horticulture at its finest. It is certainly one of the best ways to take in a tour of this attractive area.

Oxton Village, 2019.

Moreton Village

Never has a name been so appropriate for a village than that of Moreton. The Norse meaning is: 'More', a lake, and 'Ton', a town. It was once a tidal lagoon and even now 3,000 acres of Moreton are between 3 and 5 feet below sea level, with the remainder only 5 feet above sea level at most. It is little wonder that it became known as Moreton-in-the-Mud as it frequently flooded. Serious inundations came in 1912, 1918, 1924 and 1927. The 1924 flood washed away part of the bridge over the River Fender. Despite all this a large shanty town sprung up around Pasture Road and Leasowe Road at the turn of the last century as the land at that time was free of rates and attracted people to the area who built shacks and commandeered caravans to take advantage of the free land. All this freeloading came to an end when Wallasey Corporation incorporated Moreton into the borough on April Fool's Day 1928, and the council set about clearing the ramshackle property.

Despite its proclivity for flooding, the area has been utilised for more substantial buildings since Saxon times. With a population of just 165 in 1665, Moreton consisted of a small scattering of farmsteads and one public house. Long Acre Cottage was in Birkett Avenue, Richards Cottage was opposite Chapelhill Road, Dodds Cottage was sited on the corner of the current Orchard Road and Felicity Cottage was in the eponymous Felicity Grove. The pub that is Moreton's oldest was originally called the Plough Inn and Druids Arms, with the latter part of the name dropped in the 1930s. This old stone building was demolished in 1938 and replaced by a new build that survived until the end of the twentieth century; the site has now been taken by a Tesco Express. The original Farmers

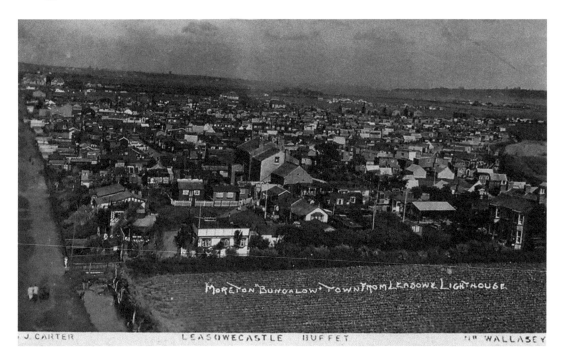

The Shanty Town at Moreton, *c.* 1925.

A bucolic scene at Moreton in 1903.

Arms dated from the late 1700s and this too was replaced by a modern building in 1934, which is still there. The third oldest pub was the Coach and Horses, which was also pulled down – this time in 1928 when a very large replacement arose directly behind. In all three cases the old pub was torn down the day before the new one opened so that the licence could be transferred overnight. The Coach and Horses became known as 'the Cathedral' because of its enormous size and it came with its own bowling green, located where Heron supermarket now stands. In the 1980s a virtual street was created inside, which operated as a Berni Inn, and numerous shops have been created on its façade. The Grange pub further west was named after the property it replaced, Grange House.

The heart of the village was centred around what is now a kidney-shaped roundabout, but was then an enclosed wooded area called The Plantation. This area was removed to facilitate traffic flow and several shops constructed on its perimeter. Those still standing to the south were constructed using money earned by the successful jockey Frank 'Tich' Mason who rode his horse Kirkland to victory in the Grand National of 1905. The winning horse's name, along with other successful mounts, had commemorative plaques erected above the shops they helped to pay for, and can still be seen today. There was an abattoir at the back of the row of shops, but it is not clear whether any of Tich's less successful horses met their end there.

The only other substantial buildings are the Church of England church on Upton Road, built on land donated by J. R. Shaw of Arrowe Hall, and the lighthouse on the nearby Moreton shore. The story that Leasowe Lighthouse was built on foundations

The Plantation at Moreton Crossroads.

Leasowe Lighthouse.

Leasowe Lighthouse,
c. 1900.

of cotton bales from a shipwreck may be apocryphal, but it does have the distinction of being the oldest brick-built lighthouse still standing in Britain. Dating from 1763, it is constructed of 660,000 hand-made bricks formed on site, with an overall height of 33 metres, consisting of seven floors reached by an internal spiral staircase. Known originally as the Upper Light, it was built in conjunction with a Lower Light, built some ¼ mile out to sea, which created a triangulation point so that mariners could navigate their vessels into the Rock Channel and thus into Liverpool. When this was washed away in a storm in 1769 a new light was built on Bidston Hill in 1771, Leasowe Lighthouse then became the new Lower Light. Its fixed beam could be seen 16 miles out to sea and protected shipping until it was finally extinguished in 1908. The keeper at this time was the widow Williams who famously brought up thirteen children in a small house adjacent to the lighthouse.

Thornton Hough Village

The picturesque village of Thornton Hough that we see today exists primarily due to the efforts of two philanthropic landlords – Joseph Hirst and William Hesketh Lever. Before their arrival the village had been described by Mortimer as 'presenting a very unpleasant appearance, and though it possesses a few tolerably good houses, the greater portion are of a very inferior description'. Mentioned in Domesday as Toritone, its present name was established when the only daughter of Roger de Thorneton, the local landowner, married Richard de Hoghe around 1320. By the nineteenth century the land was owned by Baron Mostyn of Flint.

Joseph Hirst, a wealthy textile manufacturer from Huddersfield, bought a large area to the east of the estate on a rise above the existing village and set about building a church with an accompanying vicarage, the village's first school and a row of cottages behind

A general view of Thornton Hough, looking north.

All Saints' Church, Thornton Hough.

the church that he called Wilshaw Terrace after the small Yorkshire village of his birth. Behind the Terrace he built Thornton House for himself. All were built of a distinctive rock-faced stone and present a most pleasing aspect today, especially when approached from the Neston side. All Saints' Church was built between 1867 and 1868 at a cost of £7,000 by Kirk and Sons of Huddersfield, and is unusual in having five clock faces – the fifth was placed higher up the spire to enable Mr Hirst to view it from his bedroom window. The vicarage is contemporaneous with the church and Wilshaw Terrace went up in 1870 to a design similar to almshouses Hirst had built in Wilshaw, but with a delightful conical-roofed affair at the end of the terrace to house the village post office.

The other great man in the Thornton Hough story is Lord Leverhulme, who had moved to Thornton Manor on the outskirts of the village in 1888, having recently purchased large swathes of land on the estate. He simultaneously set about improving and updating the manor and transforming the village, demolishing many of the insanitary dwellings and replacing them with half-timbered cottages and a smithy with its own spreading chestnut tree. He also built a second school and a Liberal Club, which soon became the Village Club, along with various residences to house his family. His crowning glory, however, was St George's Church, which was built in the Early English style of architecture by James Lomax-Simpson – Lever's godson. The craftsmanship displayed in the church is magnificent, built to an historical accuracy based on Lomax-Simpsons regular trips to original examples of the style throughout Britain and abroad.

During an evening's stroll through this attractive village, it is perhaps worth contemplating how the vision and philanthropic intent of just two men can create a place of such lasting beauty.

St George's Church, Thornton Hough.

Liscard Village

It is difficult to imagine Liscard ever being a village in its own right, positioned as it is today at the centre of a large dormitory town surrounded by streets of Victorian and Edwardian bay-windowed houses. There is however one amazing survivor, practically lost in the sea of housing adjoining Liscard Shopping Centre. It is a medium-sized, unassuming house on the corner of Eldon Road and Rullerton Road and gives little clue as to its former life as the farmhouse at the centre of a unique Victorian initiative, for this is the only surviving remnant of the model farm, an agricultural enterprise of international repute. Harold Littledale, the son-in-law of Sir John Tobin (more of whom later) inherited a large piece of land on Sir John's death and set about creating a farm, the likes of which had not been seen in this country before. All modern techniques and machinery were to be employed, with the best possible workmanship and implements. The farm covered over 350 acres, stretching as far as the Wallasey Golf Links, with most given over to agriculture but with a dairy herd of eighty cows kept in state-of-the-art shippons, being described by a visitor as 'well ventilated as Her Majesty's stables at Buckingham Palace'. He went on to describe the dairy as 'containing a marble fountain which would put to shame ... those recently erected in Trafalgar Square'. The farm labourers were treated quite literally less than cattle, as they were housed in lowly cottages adjacent to a large lake situated near to where St Albans Church now stands.

Steam power was still only being used on a small scale in agriculture at this time but Littledale embraced the technology, employing a newfangled steam engine to thresh the corn produced on the farm, divide the grain, grind it into flour, mix food for the pigs and,

Liscard Model Farm, *c.* 1900.

Liscard Model Farm, 2019.

last but not least, churn the butter. Farmers from far and wide and even from abroad came to view the model farm and its modern technology. Most of the farmland was gradually engulfed in housing but some of the estate survives as open land as it was eventually bought by Wallasey Council to form part of Central Park, which remains a valuable open space in the town.

At the centre of Central Park until its demolition in 2008 stood Liscard Hall, formerly Moors Hey House, the family home of Sir John Tobin, former mayor of Liverpool, privateer and owner of land, ships and slaves. Built in 1834 on a slight rise, Sir John's wife could keep an eye on the safe passage of his personal yacht on the Mersey on stormy days through a large telescope he had installed in the highest window of the hall for this purpose. It remained in the family until the land was given over for the park and the building became the town's School of Art. Nearby St John's Church was built for Sir John by Henry Turberville Edwards – his only known work. Sir John's son became the first incumbent and Tobin's last resting place is within the churchyard. Its large Doric front of Storeton stone and four-columned portico look rather forlorn at the time of writing as the church has been empty for many years, awaiting a use commensurate with its impressive architecture.

Central Park, Liscard, in 1905.

Central Park, Liscard

Liscard Hall, home of Sir John Tobin.

Bromborough Village

This is another distinct Wirral village swamped by the relentless tide of twentieth-century suburbia. It had all the elements of the traditional English village: the pub, the church, the market cross, the main street and the manorial hall. One or two of these elements endure but, as is so often the case, the essence of the place has been lost to accommodate the avaricious needs of the motor car. The most grievous losses have been in domestic architecture. Many fine large mansions along the A41 have been demolished including Brookhurst, Mendell Lodge and Bromborough Hall, practically all the farm buildings have been lost and even the Saxon church has gone, although this was torn down by Georgian philistines rather than their 1960s counterparts. Despite all this carnage the powers that be continued to push for demolition of the remaining infrastructure before the Bromborough Society stepped up to the plate and said enough is enough. Stanhope House at the edge of the village is a physical reminder that the invidious canker of modernity for its own sake can be halted and important old buildings can be saved for future generations to enjoy.

The village of Bromborough has been spelt in no fewer than eleven different ways over the years, the most evocative being Brunanburh. This was the name of the most important battle in Anglo-Saxon history prior to the Battle of Hastings in 1066. It took place in AD 937 and was fought between Aethelstan, the King of England, and a coalition of forces brought together by Olaf Guthfrithson of Scotland and Owen of Strathclyde. Aethelstan's victory preserved the unity of England and led to its consolidation as a nation state. One of two major contenders for the site of this important battle was Brunanburh on Wirral, the other being Barnston Bar near Doncaster. The site remains a matter of conjecture and a subject of lively debate.

The area has been important in the history of Wirral ever since Aethelflaeda, the daughter of no less a legend than Alfred the Great, founded a monastery here in AD 912,

Stanhope House in Bromborough.

Bromborough Village Hall.

The Cross. Bromborough.

Bromborough Village crossroads, *c.* 1910.

an event commemorated in the current church of St Barnabus. Edward I granted a charter for a fair and a market in 1278, and the base and steps of the market cross date from this period. The shaft is a much later addition and was created in 1874. Many of the farms in the village were situated near to the cross: Manor House Farm was in Allport Lane, Cross Farm and Hall Farm were both in Village Road, and Telletts Farm was in Bromborough Village Road – its farmhouse survives as a private dwelling adjacent to the Midland bank.

The most important secular building, as in most villages, was the hall, which was sited near where the Royal Oak Hotel now stands. The original Bromborough Hall was built around 1100, being rebuilt in 1617 and demolished as late as 1933. The Mainwaring family were the lords of the manor throughout this time, boasting an unbroken line of twenty-six generations and 760 years, beginning with Ranulf de Mesnilwarin, a supporter of William the Conqueror during his subjugation of the English from 1066, for which service he was amply rewarded with fifteen manors in Cheshire, including Bromborough. The Mainwaring crest – an ass's head issuing from a coronet – was built into the south front of the hall. The family finally left for their Shropshire estates in 1856.

Occupation by the Rankin and Dale families was followed by the final occupant of the hall, Sir William Bower Forwood, a well-respected Liverpool merchant and future lord mayor. Sir William did not live to see the destruction of his beautiful gardens for the Bromborough Bypass nor the destruction of the hall itself. He died in 1925.

Mention has been made of the Saxon church that was sited just to the north of the present church. Although it was demolished in 1829, twenty years before the advent of

Bromborough Hall, *c.* 1925.

St Barnabus Church, Bromborough.

photography, there is a drawing of how it looked, dating from 1809 and now residing in the British Museum. It was a basic layout of chancel and nave with a south porch and a separate entrance directly into the chancel with a Norman chevron design typical of this early period. A small wooden belfry contained a single bell. During the incumbency of Revd James Mainwaring, another member of the notable occupants of Bromborough Hall, decided that the church was beyond repair and had it knocked down. Whether this end was preferable to having it scraped and improved beyond recognition by overeager Victorian restorers is open to debate. The master of Victorian restoration, however, Sir George Gilbert Scott, was commissioned to build the replacement church, which was competed in 1863–64. Built to a cruciform design with broad aisles to north and south, the church presents a fine addition to the village, as well it might considering the large amount of money expended on it, mostly through the generosity of rich benefactors who had just started arriving in the village from the smoke and dirt of the rapidly expanding city of Liverpool.

Bidston Village

There is something otherworldly about Bidston. Its hall casts a pall over the village, brooding above the main street like a wraith in the half-light of dusk. Above the hall stands the menacing bulk of Bidston Hill, a place of dark woods and sandstone outcrops, some containing mysterious carvings of sun gods and goddesses. The aura of strange rituals and foul deeds seems to cling to the very rocks of the place, and is shunned at night by most sensible people, leaving the hall to the nocturnal ne'er-do-wells and phantoms.

Fire on Bidston Hill, *c.* 1910.

Church Farm, Bidston.

The atmosphere rapidly changes, however, where the end of the village abuts a large 1970s council estate. New house building continues apace, and they are even going up on the nearby water meadows. Though there is still much to see within the village and the surrounding area. Starting in Bidston Village Road heading east, the first buildings of note are the Grade II listed almshouses, built as late as 1901 in memory of George Clover, a shipbuilder and local resident, by his widow Emily. To the south stands Church Farm, the largest farm in the village. Dating from the seventeenth century, this Grade II listed building is mysterious even for Bidston. There is some evidence that it may have housed a community of monks at one time and the structure itself is odd indeed, with its thirteen different floor levels, traces of underground passages and a blocked-off room reached via a window, but with no other physical access or egress. The gable end alone has six windows, all of different designs and all at differing heights. The outbuildings include an old granary with weathered stone steps leading to the first floor, which once housed temporary workers brought in at harvest time. The granary was protected by the farmyard dog whose kennel was ingeniously built into the fabric of the steps.

Opposite stands Stone Farm on the corner of School Lane, named from a large millstone set into the yard wall. This building was the Ring O' Bells pub for many years and provided hospitality for a diverse clientele. As well as being the venue for the local hunt to meet, it was also a halfway house for cocklers from Hoylake bringing their catch to market at Birkenhead, and for boxers on their way to train at West Kirby. It ceased

St Oswald's Church, Bidston.

to be a pub in 1868 after numerous complaints by Lady Cust of Leasowe Castle, who was offended while attending nearby St Oswald's Church by scenes of drunkenness and debauchery, and the unedifying sight of drunken people fast asleep in the churchyard.

The tower of St Oswald's Church dates from the early sixteenth century and is very similar to the old tower of St Hilary's Church in Wallasey, which can be seen from the top. The remainder is a rebuild by W&J Hay from 1855–56 and contains several notable memorials and inscriptions, perhaps the most poignant one being a wreath sent by Queen Victoria to the funeral of Percy Cust, a fourteen-year-old page who tragically died in 1884. The war memorial within the church names the fallen from the First World War, but also mentions Phyllis Hutchinson, the daughter of the local miller who perished aboard the *Lusitania* in 1915, an atrocity that brought America nearer to war with Germany. Consecrated in the name of St Oswald following a fruitless search for the original dedication, it was so named from an old church bell that was said to have been rescued by monks at the time of the Dissolution of the Monasteries and hidden on Hilbre Island, having been acquired from St Oswald's Church in Chester.

Several smaller farms are still extant within the village: Yew Tree Farm dates from 1696 but bears evidence of an older cruck-framed building, and Ivy Farm is eighteenth century, the village green being absorbed into the front gardens of these two buildings. Lilac Farm,

Bidston Hall around 1910.

named from the profusion of lilac bushes in the front garden, was saved from dereliction in the 1980s and boasts an adjacent tithe barn some 60 feet long and 22 feet wide.

Bidston Hall rises up to the south-east of the village. First built in the sixteenth century to house members of the Stanley family and guests on their occasional hunts on Bidston Hill, it was greatly enlarged by William Stanley, the 6th Earl of Derby who was the first lord of the manor to actually live in the hall. It was nearly lost in the 1930s due to neglect but was lovingly restored back to its former glory by a Mr and Mrs Faulkner. What excites architectural historians is the fact that the hall is entered centrally, not at the low end as was the norm, thus making it a very early example of Renaissance planning.

Above the hall stands Bidston Hill, 40 acres of woods and sandstone outcrops bought off Henry Vyner and opened as a public space in 1894. It has more than its fair share of interesting buildings, beginning in the north with Bidston Lighthouse. Built in 1872 of rock-faced stone, it replaced one of 1771 and was the upper light of a pair, indicating the correct position for shipping to enter the Rock Channel and onward to Liverpool Docks. It was used during the Napoleonic Wars as a lookout for approaching French vessels and again during the Second World War to look out for German warplanes. The actual light was extinguished in 1913 although it has been reinstated recently. The Bidston Observatory shares the same enclosure as the lighthouse and was built in 1866 after the original facility based at Waterloo was deemed ineffective due to the poor air quality in Liverpool. It was constructed of sturdy rock-faced stone to minimise any vibrations

Bidston Observatory.

that could have affected the delicate instruments within. The Tidal Institute moved here in 1929 and gained worldwide acclaim for the accuracy and efficiency of their tidal predictions. It was here that the tides for D-Day in 1944 were worked out, playing a vital role in the success of the invasion.

Stretching from the observatory to the windmill there once stood a novel signalling system that indicated the arrival of ships into Liverpool. Built in 1763 by interested Liverpool shipowners, the system consisted of nearly eighty flagpoles with various shipping lines' house flags, which would be hoisted when a ship of that line entered the Channel. Some of the holes for the flagpoles can still be seen cut into the sandstone. This operation was superseded by a line of eight semaphore stations stretching from Anglesey to Bidston, which could report the arrival of ships off Holyhead to the port of Liverpool in just five minutes from 75 miles away. This was in turn superseded by an electric telegraph system, which connected Holyhead directly to Liverpool by cable.

A short walk along the ridge brings us to Bidston windmill, the latest of several mills built on this site since 1600. The original mill was burnt down in 1791, with subsequent rebuilds and repairs after major fires in 1821 and again in 1839. Fire was a major hazard for mills; if the sails were not firmly secured before stormy weather there was always a risk of them breaking free and causing a catastrophic fire due to the friction produced. The site of the original mill can still be made out 20 metres north of the current mill, which local soap manufacturer R. S. Hudson had fully restored in 1894. It may be visited on open days organised each year by Wirral Leisure Services.

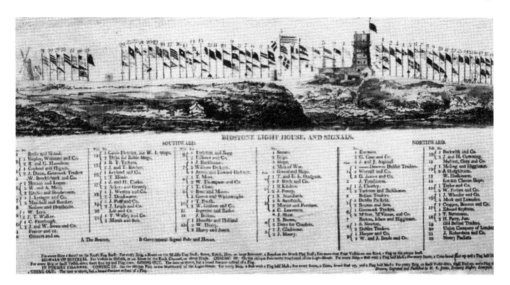

The original lighthouse and flag system on Bidston Hill, 1850.

Bidston Windmill around 1900.

One of Bidston's better-kept secrets are the series of tunnels below the hill constructed during the Second World War as air-raid shelters. These are quite substantial and contained over 2,000 bunks, a canteen, staff dormitory, medical aid post and a ventilation shaft that could double as an emergency escape route. It was proposed that they could be used in the event of nuclear attack in the Cold War, but when this danger faded the entrance near Hoylake Road was permanently sealed up, although some intrepid souls still manage to squeeze in for a look around.

Just off the Hill are several more interesting and historical buildings. During the vast expansion of Birkenhead in the 1850s and 1860s the Birkenhead Commissioners built a large water tower and a cemetery nearby. The tower is 50 feet high and was completed in 1865 together with an adjacent reservoir. Recent house construction has not lessened its grandeur on such a prominent site. Flaybrick Hill Cemetery to the north was constructed from an old quarry in the usual imposing Victorian way by Edward Kemp, with serpentine paths, Gothic lodges and chapels and ostentatious memorials to local worthies. Steps have been made to preserve the fabric of the cemetery from vandalism, although the ivy-strewn Gothic architecture somehow lends itself to semi-dereliction. Across Boundary Road lies Tam O'Shanter Cottage, originally constructed by a heath squatter and named after a character in the poem by Robert Burns, which has been carved into a stone slab on the side of the building.

Tam O'Shanter Cottage, Bidston.

One final building of note is no longer in Bidston. Soap manufacturer Robert Hudson decided that the beautiful mansion he had built for himself in 1891, then called Bidston Court, did not have a nice enough view, so he had the entire house moved brick by brick across Wirral to Royden Park in Frankby. The entire enterprise took three years – from 1928 to 1931. He renamed it Hill Bark and it still resides in its more sylvan setting today as a popular hotel.

DID YOU KNOW?
The 6th Earl of Derby, a member of the wealthy Stanley family and owner of Bidston Hall, brought William Shakespeare to Bidston as a member of a band of actors. The playwright stayed at Bidston Hall for several days.

Willaston Village

Walking through Willaston today, it is hard to imagine that it was once the most important village in Wirral. The village green was far larger than it is now, including a rectangular area now covered by the Memorial Hall, Willaston Green Mews, Cherry Brow Terrace and the Pollard Inn. This uniquely large area was used as a place of assembly for the hundred of Wilaveston. The hundred covered an area larger than Wirral, with five additional townships, each sending reeves and other worthies to the hundred court, or wapentake as it was then known, where matters of taxation, administration and the proclamation of royal decrees all took place on the green. The green is now a fraction of its original size but still forms the focal point of the village. The most notable building extant is the former Red Lion Hotel. Built as a single private dwelling, it was occupied as two cottages in the eighteenth century before being joined together again and becoming licensed premises. In 1928 the building ceased to be a public house and returned to being a private dwelling. However, in 1962 its peace was disturbed again when Birkenhead Brewery applied to pull the building down and replace it with a modern pub. Considering the sort of heinous modernist eyesores that masqueraded as architecture in the 1960s, it is lucky that planning permission was refused and the property was allowed to return to its slumbers. Another pub in the village that has had a less eventful life is The Nags Head. Formerly known as The White Horse, it has stood near to the green since 1738, although the fabric of the building has changed substantially over the years.

To the east of the green, Hadlow Road runs south past Willaston Old Hall to an unused level crossing that now crosses the Wirral Way – a 13-mile-long linear country park that opened in 1973 and follows the route of the old Hooton to West Kirby Railway. A glance to the left produces the unexpected vista of a disused railway station. Hadlow Road station (so called to avoid confusion with another Willaston station in Cheshire, near Crewe), has been lovingly restored and preserved to its 1950s glory by an enthusiastic team of volunteers who work tirelessly to retain this reminder of the bygone age of steam railways for future generations. Opened on 1 October 1886 by the Birkenhead

The Red Lion at Willaston.

Joint Railway as a branch line of the Birkenhead to Chester line, it ran from Hooton to Parkgate with one other stop at Neston, with its original *raison d'être* being to service the colliery there. It was further extended to West Kirby on 19 April 1886 to benefit from the burgeoning tourist trade. Despite its popularity it was only ever a single line affair with passing loops, as can be seen at Hadlow Road where a short length of track has been relaid. Despite setbacks such as the closure of Neston Colliery in 1927, the line continued until 17 September 1956 for passengers and 7 May 1962 for freight, with the line being lifted in 1964. The principal remaining buildings are all on the eastern (down) platform and form a most picturesque group. The old ticket office is now a small atmospheric museum and the signal box has been recently renovated, although this is not the original, this one having been dismantled and moved to Hadlow Road from Hassall Green on the North Staffordshire Railway. A K6 telephone box adds a splash of colour to the scene. It would take a singular lack of imagination not to be able to conjure up visions of waiting on the platform for the 2:15 to Hooton after purchasing your ticket in the ticket office nearby, then watching the engine steaming into view and the sulphurous smell in the nostrils as it slows to a stop at the platform with a satisfying hiss.

To the north of the village, along a winding country lane appropriately named Mill Lane, stands Wirral's largest windmill. Its sails are gone, destroyed in a storm in 1930, but at 80 feet high it is still an impressive structure. Classified as Grade II by English Heritage, it was constructed in 1800 on the site of a previous mill. Built in five stages, it still retains much of the original machinery, which rotated the cap within its upper stage. In its heyday

Hadlow Road station.

Willaston Mill.

when owned by the Radford family of Liverpool, it had ten millstones producing flour, four utilising the power of the wind via the large sails, and six driven by a steam engine installed for the purpose. The Radfords massively expanded the business, building a large bakery on the site and acquiring two ships that imported grain into Birkenhead Docks from the Russian Steppe. They even bought a steam traction engine to move the grain from Birkenhead to Willaston. Steam, however, was to prove the downfall of this enterprise as huge steam-driven mills installed at the docks made Birkenhead the largest milling area in the world. When the sails were destroyed in 1930 the windmill ceased production and fell into gradual decline. It has since been renovated and is now a private dwelling.

Bebington Village

Named after a Saxon chieftain named Bebba, Bebington has always been separated into an upper and lower village. Lower Bebington was always the most important of the two as it was once on the main stagecoach route from Chester to Birkenhead with up to thirty coaches passing through each day. As was usual in these circumstances several public houses sprung up to cater for the travellers, and many of these hostelries have survived. The Travellers Rest and the Rose and Crown remain relatively unchanged – the latter dates from 1730 and was built on the site of an even older inn. There was a small inn named the Royal Oak located in Village Road dating from 1739; it closed its doors for good in 1960 and is now business premises. When a large pub called The Acorn was built nearby, it gave rise to the saying 'From a tiny Oak, a mighty Acorn grew'. One other hostelry of note in the area is Kings Arms, not The Kings Arms as most people erroneously call it; it is named after a local landowner called King.

Bebington Village, looking east.

The Lower Village had numerous farms and smallholdings, one of which, Old Hall Farm, survives as the local branch of the Royal British Legion. Another notable survivor is the large thatched property in The Grove. Known locally as 'The Thatch' and dating from 1656, its survival is principally due to the road being diverted away from the cottage in 1840. At one time it was owned by the council and became the oldest council house in Wirral. More substantial houses were built in Bebington, chief among them being Bebington Old Hall, which was built in the 1830s and at one time acted as the rectory for nearby St Andrew's Church. Brackenwood House was designed by Sir Aston Webb, best known as the designer of Buckingham Palace, for the Evans family. Later owners were the Jacob family of cracker fame before a spell as council offices. Edgeworth House is the only one that survives and was the home of Charlotte (Lottie) Dod, who was such a remarkable sportswoman that *The Guinness Book of Records* honoured her with the accolade of 'Most Versatile Female Athlete of All Time'. Little wonder as her achievements included being

Lottie Dod at the London Olympics, 1908.

St Andrew's Church, Bebington.

Wimbledon Ladies Singles Champion five times, the first when she was only fifteen; British Ladies Amateur Golf Champion; and Olympic Archery silver medallist in 1908. She also played field hockey for England, tobogganed down the Cresta Run, figure skated at world-class level and was a keen mountaineer. What this redoubtable lady did in her spare time has not been recorded.

Other famous residents include Joseph Mayer, who provided the town with Mayer Park, Mayer Library and its 10,000 books, Mayer Hall and much else. Then there was the eccentric stonemason Thomas Francis, whose strange cryptic engravings known as the Puzzle Stones attracted the opprobrium of Nathaniel Hawthorne who 'puzzled over their cryptic inscriptions' and suggested they were the work of 'some half-crazy person'. Sir Harold Wilson gets a footnote as a former pupil of Wirral Grammar School.

The only Grade I listed building in Bebington is St Andrew's Church. Built predominantly of wood by the Saxons in the tenth century, it was rebuilt of local light Storeton stone in the fourteenth century and was known as the 'White Church'. The steeple dates from this time and its great height must have been quite a landmark in the area, so much so that it was reported Oliver Cromwell's troops used it as target practice when they camped on Abbotts Grange. Rightly described as one of the finest churches in Wirral, its varied architecture both inside and out merely adds to its appeal, a product of numerous building campaigns from Saxon, through Tudor to Victorian times, although restoration in the 1800s caused much loss of original fabric.

Former tramway cottages, Cross Lane, Bebington.

Upper Bebington was dominated by the quarries beside Mount Road, which had been producing fine white Storeton stone since Roman times. Many of the cottages and terraces in the area were built to house the quarry workers who extracted the stone for many of the local landmarks, including Birkenhead Town Hall, St Andrew's Church and Storeton Hall. It was a major source of stone for the Liverpool to Manchester Railway and was even utilised as facing stone on the Empire State Building in New York. At its apogee it was 200 feet deep, covering an area of some 9 acres. The demand for Storeton stone had always outstripped supply due to the problems of transporting it by road when the carriageways were little more than rutted dirt tracks. It was not uncommon for the 2-mile journey from quarry to dockside to take three weeks, ripping up existing roads as it went. This problem was overcome with the construction of the Storeton Tramway. Built between 1837 and 1838 it improved the haulage time from three weeks to two hours. Flat wagons were loaded with stone and sent down towards the terminus at Bromborough Dock by gravity, the empty wagons being hauled back to the quarry by horsepower. Although most of the tramway route has been obliterated, there is still evidence of the route to look out for. Where the tracks crossed Rest Hill Road two of the stone gateposts remain in situ. The track then passed under Mount Road via a tunnel which is now full of detritus but can just about be made out through the undergrowth. The track then emerged north of Bracken Lane before crossing the lane further down. No evidence remains until it reaches the playing fields of Wirral Grammar School where the route can be discerned as a stretch of darker grass on the playing field. Two engineers' houses known as Firtree Cottages survive in Cross Lane where the track passed to the south, evidenced by two remaining gateposts on the east side of Cross Lane. Quarry Avenue and Quarry Road East mark the route now before the final extant feature: the tunnel under the railway line, which is now a footpath leading to Port Sunlight. The track ran in front of Levers factory and down to the stone jetty at Bromborough Pool.

DID YOU KNOW?
Thomas Francis, 'the Bebington Eccentric', utilised his skills as a stonemason by digging his own grave and lining it with stone. He enjoyed nothing more than sitting in it for hours on end, smoking his pipe.

4. Smugglers and Wreckers – Desperate Times on the Wild Wirral Coast

Between the fourteenth and the end of the nineteenth centuries nearly all seaside communities in Britain made a substantial income or even a living from smuggling. The coasts of Devon and Cornwall are the best-known areas for this nefarious activity, but the majority of people on the north and west Wirral coasts also had a reputation as enthusiastic smugglers. Heavy duties had been imposed on imported goods ever since Edward I placed tariffs on wool imports from the Continent to finance the Hundred Years' War. With each successive increase in customs duties the propensity to indulge in smuggling became ever more attractive, eventually reaching industrial proportions.

James Stonehouse wrote in his book *Recollections of Old Liverpool* (1863):

> Wirral up to the middle of the 18th Century was a desperate region. The inhabitants were nearly all wreckers and smugglers. They ostensibly carried on a trade or calling of fishermen, farm labourers and small farmers ... [but] scarcely a house in North Wirral could not provide a guest with a good stiff glass of brandy or Hollands [Geneva or gin].

Heswall Beach at sunset, *c.* 1935.

Throughout most of the seventeenth century most smuggled goods came to Wirral from the Isle of Man – Manx customs duties being extremely low. Contraband was sent in small fast boats to Wallasey on the east coast and to Heswall and Gayton in west Wirral. This continued until the British government bought the lordship of Man for £27,000 in 1765, which put a stop to the trade. Ever-resourceful, however, the smugglers then turned to Ireland to provide them with goods. The bulk of the gangs held down normal jobs and used smuggling as a way to increase their meagre incomes. The occupations of many lent themselves to this illegal trade: fishermen who provided boats to bring contraband ashore, farmers to move the stuff inland, innkeepers to sell the spirits and tobacco, and tailors to utilise the silks and muslin. There were in practice two types of smuggler: the sea smuggler and the land smuggler. The former transferred the goods from ships offshore onto the beach and the latter moved contraband to hiding places or straight to end users. The scale of all this mischief is revealed by an auction flyer of the time that advertised the sale of recovered contraband. Included in the sale were 144 gallons of brandy, 39 gallons of rum, 25 lb of tea and a pound of coffee.

DID YOU KNOW?
One of the many small caves dotted throughout New Brighton emerged in a cellar in Wellington Road, which was often flooded by seawater to a depth of 7 feet. This was inhabited by a sea creature – probably an octopus. Christened 'Higgledy', it was treated as a pet by the eccentric owner who fed it rats, chickens and eventually his own dog. His understandably apprehensive children moved out soon afterwards.

Wirral at this time was a collection of small communities, each of them related (not always in a good way), each of them poor, and each with a collective *laissez faire* outlook to breaking the law – rather like people's attitudes to the Black Market in the Second World War and bootlegging in the United States in the 1920s. Times were hard. Innkeepers could not always scratch a living selling beer and taking in lodgers; an extra income therefore made perfect sense as the chances of being caught by the small band of customs officials was minimal, especially as their responsibilities included not just patrolling the beaches but inspecting ships moored offshore as well.

Most landings of contraband were small, being removed from ships and taken from the beaches often before the customs men were aware of their presence. These took place predominantly on Gayton and Heswall beaches as Parkgate was too open and had its own customs house. The land smugglers took the booty to secluded places where they were hidden overnight rather than being taken to an inn where the customs may have been watching. Their tracks were covered by the local farmers who drove cattle over the pathways to obscure any evidence of their nocturnal activities. Popular landing places were at the foot of Manners Lane or in the secluded areas around Heswall Common, such as the

Old smugglers' path at Thurstaston, *c.* 1935.

The Cave in Thurstaston Road, Heswall.

Dungeon, the Dales and the Beacon. Locals even invented stories of ghosts and headless horsemen to scare off the inquisitive. Goods were often secreted in caves; some were natural features but many were hewn out of the soft sandstone by the smugglers themselves. Near one of these caves a Liverpool fruit merchant, James Adam, had a rock-faced mansion built for his family and called it The Cave. It is still here today. Others are said to survive around Irby Hall and Thurstaston Hall. Occasionally larger shipments were landed, organised by 'Mr Bigs', who often turned out to be magistrates or customs officials. These were moved directly to Chester where the goods were dispersed and the money divvied up. So much money was made in smuggling that the proceeds could not be used for the purchase of local properties for fear of bringing attention to themselves. The cash was either kept or property was bought from outside the area. One smuggler left four houses in Liverpool in his will along with £800 to provide for his granddaughters – a colossal sum in those days. All this activity was classed as smuggling. The practice of wrecking is quite another thing and a definition here is appropriate: 'WRECKING: The practice of taking valuables from a shipwreck which has foundered or run aground close to shore.'

There is an urban myth that wreckers deliberately decoyed ships on to coasts by the use of false lights so that they would run ashore for easy plundering. There is no clear

The former Ring O' Bells Inn at Bidston.

evidence that this ever happened. Such subterfuges would not have worked in any case as mariners interpret lights as indicating land and so avoid them if they cannot identify them. Smuggling, however, was another matter and was just as prevalent on the north and east shores of the peninsula as it was in Heswall and Gayton. The undisputed epicentre of the gangs on this side of Wirral was Mother Redcaps, run by an unattractive but trustworthy Cheshire woman called Poll Jones who always wore a red bonnet, giving the tavern its popular nickname, although it was at the time actually called the Halfway House. Patrons of the hostelry were predominantly mariners who entrusted their money to Polly when they went away to sea.

Built in 1595 on a desolate and isolated spot on the Wallasey shoreline, the inn was a small two-storey affair with walls 3 feet thick to withstand the winter storms that raged along the coast. A heavy oak door 5 inches thick guarded the entrance, which also boasted thick sliding cross bars that were secured into the stone frame. If this wasn't enough protection, just behind the door lay an intricate apparatus that opened up a trapdoor if the door was forced open, precipitating the intruder into the 9-foot cellar. On quieter days it doubled as the beer cellar. Because of its remote position it was the ideal place to bring smuggled goods, and there were many places within the fabric of the building that could secrete booty for collection at a later date. There are abundant stories of smugglers outwitting the customs men with various ruses. One such tale involves the efforts to remove a customs officer from Mother Redcaps so

Egremont Promenade and Mother Redcaps, 1905.

that contraband could be taken away from the inn. It was arranged that one of the gang would creep down to the shore and lie down in his clothes in the water. The attention of the officer was called to the supposed body that had been washed ashore, and sure enough he ran onto the beach and began rifling through his pockets in an attempt to identify the corpse. At this the man sprang up and laid out the officer, giving the rest of the gang time to remove their ill-gotten gains from the inn and onwards towards Bidston.

DID YOU KNOW?
There is an old Wallasey prayer that sums up the attitude of the majority of people on the north Wirral shore at the time: 'God Bless Father and God Bless Mother, and God send us a wreck afore morning.'

As in Heswall there was an abundance of natural and man-made caves in the vicinity where goods could be hidden. Many of these caves have been partially explored but no comprehensive study has been made to ascertain exactly how many there are and where they all lead. There are stories of caves running inland for miles and connecting

Mother Redcaps around 1930.

up with various landmarks, caves are meant to lead from Mother Redcaps to the cave systems at the Red and Yellow Noses and the system of caves discovered under the Palace Amusement Park, which were utilised during the Second World War as a munitions factory, or as far as St Hilary's Church and Bidston. There was even talk of caves linking up to Chester Castle, but this seems most unlikely as it is some 18 miles away. Some of these caves were indeed large, the strangely named Wormhole at Yellow Noses in New Brighton is probably the largest known and contains graffiti from as early as 1619 incised into the sandstone walls. Access to all of these caves has now been bricked up or totally obliterated with infill and landfalls over the decades.

The most likely scenario involving smuggling in Wallasey appears to be the landing of contraband from ships anchored in the Mersey opposite Mother Redcaps at a place called Red Betts Pool. A dummy weathervane attached to a large seat made of ship timber outside the inn indicated whether it was safe to land stolen goods: if the vane pointed to the inn all was well, but if pointing towards the river it was the sign to stay away. If the coast was clear, the goods were landed and taken away by packhorse across Liscard Moor, which abutted the shore, over to Liscard Village and then over the dreary moor, which lay between the Boot Inn in Liscard and the Breck, a quarry along Wallasey Ridge, then across Bidston Moss, a treacherous marshy area criss-crossed with inlets and pools and no place for anyone not *au fait* with the one narrow pathway that led across to Bidston Village and the final destination, the Ring O' Bells Inn. At the most dangerous part of the path a pair of whale jaw bones had been placed across one of

The Red Noses at New Brighton around 1900.

The original coastline at New Brighton.

the inlets with boards laid across to make a rudimentary bridge. Again, stories were propagated of ghosts and ghouls to scare away the curious, although it would have been strange for anyone to have wanted to be here without good reason as it was a fog-bound and miserable spot at any time.

The advent of free trade in the 1840s put an end to most smuggling activities, but Mother Redcaps soldiered on for another 120 years before being demolished in 1974, ending an interesting but illicit chapter in the history of Wirral.

DID YOU KNOW?

Smuggling is a crime created entirely by governments, being as old as the first tax or regulation on trade. In the eighteenth century tea, tobacco, spices, silks and spirits were smuggled into England in quantities exceeding those brought in legitimately.

5. The Peoples Garden – The Story of Birkenhead's Historic Park

The meteoric rise of Birkenhead from the beginning of the nineteenth century is a reflection on the state of the United Kingdom during these revolutionary years. The Industrial Revolution was in full swing and was about to receive a massive boost with the advent of the railways, which were to prove the defining invention of the century. Birkenhead had expanded from a few cottages and an old priory on the coastal strip to a large industrial town with aspirations of being a rival to Liverpool just across the river. Fine houses were put up around Hamilton Square and the intention was to fill the surrounding streets with equally fine villas and mansions for the burgeoning middle classes. The reality unfortunately did not measure up to the ideal due to several financial slumps, with smaller houses being built to fill up the preprepared roads on what became known as the gridiron.

As a buffer to the onward march of housing and as a much-needed green space in a sea of bricks and mortar, it was proposed to lay out a large public park on a scale that befitted

Northern Block at Hamilton Square, looking west.

the aspirations of the town grandees. One of these grandees and a leading advocate of the park was Sir William Jackson, a baronet, Liberal politician and Member of Parliament, railway entrepreneur and wealthy businessman, having made his money in palm oil from Africa. He resided nearby in Claughton Manor and as a prominent voice on the Board of Local Improvement Commissioners for the town, his forceful advocacy led to a Private Act of Parliament in 1843 giving Royal Assent for the construction of a large public park to be paid for out of public expense – the very first park in the world to be financed in this way. Sir William Jackson was well connected and managed to attract the services of Sir Joseph Paxton, one of the foremost landscape designers of his age who was formerly the Head Gardener at Chatsworth House and famously the designer of the Crystal Palace in Hyde Park which drew on his expertise gleaned from his designs for a large glasshouse at Chatsworth. He had already designed Princes Park in Liverpool as a privately funded enterprise in 1842 and despite initial doubts as to the prospect of building a park on such an unpromising site, he took the commission as somewhat of a challenge.

A total of 226 acres of very poor-quality, marshy ground was obtained from local landowner F. R. Price at 1s (5p) per square yard. The overall cost of the land was £69,690 (when the advantages of owning building land on the periphery of the park became apparent the price rocketed to 11s 4d (57p) a yard). Paxton's plans envisaged splitting the land into two distinct parts, with 125 acres allocated for public use and the remainder being earmarked for private housing, which would pay for the construction and running

The Boathouse in Birkenhead Park.

Cannon Hill Terrace in Park Road South.

costs of the new park. The housing would be of the highest quality Storeton stone or red and yellow brick, with both individual villas, pairs and rows of superior terracing angled in such a way as to provide owners with an unobscured view of the park. Of the 800 houses drawn on the original plan, unfortunately over half were never built. Many of the planned terraces and crescents did not materialise either. His largest groups were to be in Park Road North where Birkenhead General Hospital was eventually built, and in Park Road West where Seeley Avenue and Cranbourne Avenue now stand. The main terraced block would have stood where Birkenhead Rugby Club now have their pitches. Of those built, the villas predating the 1860s were the most in accord with Paxton's overall vision. Fine examples of individual villas remain in Ashville Road, Cavendish Road and Park Road South, with the best surviving terrace being at Cannon Hill.

To realise Paxton's plans the first job was to drain the low-lying marsh, which needed to be accomplished before any landscaping could commence. This took nearly a year and was followed by several more years moving around many tons of earth to create the Upper and Lower Lakes, with the spoil being utilised to create many of the hills and a rockery. Serpentine paths were laid down throughout the park with the largest being Park Drive, designed on the periphery specifically for vehicular traffic, predominantly the bourgeoisie in their landaus at the time. This form of irregular landscaping had become popular through the work of Capability Brown and the Romantic Movement as a rejection of the more

The Swiss Bridge in the Lower Park.

formal, rigid gardens previously designed to embellish the surroundings of the country houses of the aristocracy. Paxton brought in Edward Kemp to supervise the building work, which he continued to do in his capacity as park superintendent for the next forty-six years.

The park is separated into the Upper Park towards Claughton village, and the Lower Park towards the town. Each has its own lake with a central island and serpentine walks and footbridges. The Lower Lake also boasts the Swiss Bridge, the only covered bridge of traditional wooden construction in the United Kingdom, and a Roman boathouse, formerly doubling as a bandstand before a better-placed and larger one was built to the west of the lake.

DID YOU KNOW?
During the Second World War most of the ornate railings surrounding Birkenhead Park were removed, ostensibly to be reused for the war effort but mainly as a morale booster. The majority of the iron was unsuitable for this purpose and most of it was allegedly dumped into Liverpool Bay. The Crimean War cannons on Cannon Hill met the same fate.

Eight splendid lodges were built at the various entrances to the park, all built by the magnificently named Lewis Hornblower, together with the rather more prosaically named John Robertson. By far the grandest is the main entrance at the north-east corner, which consists of two lodges linked by a triple-arcaded screen and boasting a giant order of unfluted Ionic columns. Built to resemble a triumphal arch, this fine piece of architecture has been designated II* by English Heritage. At the southern end of Park Road East stands the Gothic Lodge, which is not Gothic but Elizabethan and is the largest of the lesser lodges. Moving west, the Italian Lodge is sited on Park Road South and is the most pleasing of the lodges with its splendid belvedere tower. Edward Hubbard, who assisted Nikolaus Pevsner in writing the Cheshire edition of the Buildings of England series of books, wrote of the Italian Lodge: 'The detailing is of the greatest sensitivity and refinement.' Further west again is the Castellated Lodge, aptly named as almost everything on it is castellated, including the chimneys. There are a pair of lodges in Park Road North named the Norman Lodges (East and West) but neither are Norman, both being built in a Greek Revivalist style with Doric porches *in antis.* One final lodge can be seen in Ashville Road, Central Lodge is a cubical pilastered affair with a rusticated ground floor.

Many popular pursuits were catered for in the park. Besides angling in the lakes, grounds were laid out for archery, crown green bowling, tennis and quoits, along with two cricket grounds with attendant pavilions – the one built in 1848 to the south of the Lower Park is one of the oldest such structures surviving in the United Kingdom. At one time there was a third lake in the Lower Park, which was popular in the winter months as a skating rink due to its shallow depth. This was eventually filled in and became a sunken garden. Other notable landmarks were the William Jackson Memorial Fountain, an obelisk of polished granite constructed in 1860; Royden House, a fine villa that became a nurses home for the nearby General Hospital; and a fine palm house, no doubt inspired by Paxton's previous glasshouses.

The grand opening in April 1847 was delayed to coincide with the opening of the Great Float Docks complex when the whole town took the day off to celebrate. Officially opened by Lord Morpeth, 10,000 revellers enjoyed such games as chasing the greasy pig and climbing the greasy pole – grease was a popular commodity in Victorian times. Hundreds of events have taken place since, notably the Welsh Eisteddfod, which came to the park in 1878, 1879 and 1917. The latter occasion was graced or otherwise by the presence of David Lloyd George, the Liberal prime minister, and the event was commemorated with a large inscribed stone. Coronations have traditionally been marked with the planting of trees, there being trees for Edward VII and Georges V and VI. Elizabeth II got the full works, however, with an avenue of lime trees being planted by local children in her honour.

Birkenhead Park was awarded a Grade I historic landscape listing in 1995 and has been voted one of the best six parks in the world, alongside the Bois de Boulogne in France, Friedrich Wilhelmsgarten in Germany, Akahi Park in Japan, Melbournes Botanic Gardens and Central Park in New York, which most people know was based on the designs for Birkenhead Park, having inspired US landscape architect Frederick Olmsted on his visit to the town. An £11 million restoration and renovation in the 2000s has greatly improved the park and it remains a valuable green oasis amidst the urban sprawl.

DID YOU KNOW?
In October 1942 Sergeant Douglas Goudie of the Royal Canadian Air Force was forced to bail out of his malfunctioning Spitfire during a test flight over Dingle in Liverpool, suffering nothing more than a sprained ankle on landing. The plane continued on, however, crossing the river and crashing in Birkenhead Park where it lay buried and forgotten until 2007 when the Warplane Wreck Investigation Group dug it up and sent the engine and other parts to Fort Perch Rock where they were put on display.

The Italian Lodge in Park Road South.

The drill hall in Grange Road West.

The main entrance to Birkenhead Park.

6. The Leisure Peninsula – Sports and Recreation on the Wirral

Wirral was designated 'the Leisure Peninsula' by Wirral Leisure Services in the 1980s and is a richly deserved title. Reform of working hours through various Victorian Factory Acts ensured that a greater proportion of employees secured a shorter working week and greater holiday entitlements, and with this came a commensurate demand for amusements. Entrepreneurs were happy to oblige, managing to fulfil the needs of an increasingly sophisticated public by remaining ahead of the curve through novelty and innovation. This is most evident in the entertainment industry where theatre impresarios brought new forms of enjoyment to the masses. From the outset theatres were not just the home of worthy dramatic productions, they offered variety shows, circus acts, music hall, dancing and song, and latterly moving pictures, which shocked and enthralled their audiences.

The first purpose-built theatre in Birkenhead was the Queens Hall Theatre, which was built in 1862. It was situated in Claughton Road where a multistorey car park adjacent to the bus station now stands. It operated solely as a theatre until 1908 when animated pictures were first shown. The theatre closed in 1912 but reopened a year later as the Queens Cinema, managing to hold its own until the massive Ritz cinema was opened on the opposite corner.

The Avenue Super Cinema, Bidston Avenue, Birkenhead.

The end came in 1949 when the first theatre in Birkenhead closed its doors and was finally pulled down in 1968. The Claughton Music Hall missed being the first theatre in Birkenhead by a matter of days, having also opened in 1862 with a charity event in aid of Birkenhead General Hospital. Designed by famous local architect Walter Scott, it was situated on the corner of the now lost Atherton Street and Claughton Road at a cost of £4,000. It took the path of many theatres in that it started as a theatre, changed to a cinema and ended as a bingo hall before demolition in 1982, changing its name several times in the process. Its days as a cinema saw it named naturally enough The Claughton Picture House and latterly The Astor before a brief flirtation with foreign films when it was The Continental. It became the Astor Tombola as early as 1957, becoming Birkenhead's first bingo hall before closure in 1981.

DID YOU KNOW?
In the early years of West Kirby Baths, the last night of the season was known as 'Mad Night', and for good reason. Men would dress up, perform comedy acts, and rampage through the women's changing rooms, throwing any unfortunate woman they encountered into the water.

The Claughton Theatre, Atherton Street, Birkenhead.

Next to arrive was the rather grand Theatre Royal, which stood in Argyle Street directly to the south of the current Wetherspoon's pub. Built by the redoubtable Lewis Hornblower (see Chapter 5), it opened in 1864 to a packed house of 1,600 souls who were entertained by a burlesque show. After over fifty successful years as a theatre it was converted to a 976-seat cinema in 1921, complete with a Greek Revivalist auditorium and a brand-new organ, renamed as the Scala. Completely demolished and rebuilt as a 2,100-seater cinema in 1937, it closed in 1982, reopening as a snooker hall and then a gym.

The most famous theatre in Birkenhead opened on 21 December 1868. At a cost of £10,000 the Argyle Theatre of Varieties opened with a full music hall bill. An admirer at the time commented that 'this new and elegant place of amusement was opened for the first time on Monday 21st inst. The Hall is seventy feet in length by forty-five feet wide...with galleries capable of seating five hundred people, the body of the Hall accommodating a similar number.' Also available were eight American bowling alleys and a large billiard room. It changed its name to The Prince of Wales Theatre in 1876 when the proscenium was enlarged, but reverted back to The Argyle in 1890 when music hall and variety filled the bill once more. Sir Harry Lauder began his long and successful career treading the boards at The Argyle, while other noteworthy performers included Dan Leno, George Roby, Vesta Tilley, Charlie Chaplin, Bud Flannagan and Stan Laurel before he teamed up with Oliver Hardy. The Argyle was the first theatre to host radio broadcasts via short-wave radio to the Commonwealth and the only one to broadcast to the USA. It was also the first outside London to show Thomas Edison's early Vitagraph

The Gaumont Cinema, Park Road East, Birkenhead.

ARGYLE STREET, BIRKENHEAD. B.H.12.

The Argyle Theatre, Argyle Street, Birkenhead.

moving pictures. The main programme, however, always revolved around live theatre, variety and music hall. The end came for this fine theatre on 21 September 1940 when the building took a direct hit from a German bomb and was totally destroyed by the resultant fire. The site eventually became a car park.

One other establishment predates the arrival of the first theatre outside Birkenhead. The Tranmere Music Hall in Old Chester Road opened on Saturday 15 November 1879 with a concert, but for most of its early life it was used as a venue for political and public meetings, due partly to its 1,200-seat capacity. After a name change to The Coliseum around 1904 it became an early adopter of moving pictures, which mainly consisted of local events shot by the proprietor and shown between theatrical performances. The 'Colly' followed a similar route to other establishments in moving on to 'talkies' before closing as a cinema in 1962 and acting as a furniture warehouse before its demolition in 2005 to make way for flats.

Wallasey was a late adopter of the mass-entertainment centres popular in Birkenhead, but when they finally built their first establishment in 1885 they really went to town. Opened as The Gaiety, it contained a grand hall and concert hall, a skating rink, an aquarium and an aviary for good measure. Unfortunately, all these attractions were housed under a corrugated-iron roof and the interior décor and seating left a lot to be desired. Custom soon fell away, especially when the Tower Theatre and its myriad superior attractions were constructed nearby. A change of name to the Palace and Pavilion Theatre and the inclusion of moving pictures failed to halt its decline and it closed in December

The Coliseum Cinema, Old Chester Road, Rock Ferry.

1926. Following demolition, the New Palace Amusement Park was built in the art deco style popular at the time, and this fine building survives to this day. The Tower Theatre was the next major theatre in the town, built beneath the mighty New Brighton Tower and dwarfing every other structure in the country. Opened in 1898 as the Tower Theatre and Circus, it seated a massive 2,000 patrons with standing room for a further 500 (see Chapter 1). It opened with a variety show with singing, dancing and real lions. Grand Opera and Sunday concerts were performed for a more refined audience. The Tower was a very early adopter of silent movies, showing some of the first Royal Bioscope films in 1904. Cinema productions took over from live performances in the main from 1930, interspersed with wrestling bouts, which proved a popular draw. Like many places of entertainment in the 1950s and '60s the Tower saw a major slump in attendances due predominantly to the popularity of television, a massive fire in 1969 led to its destruction.

DID YOU KNOW?
At the beginning of the nineteenth century an old guide to Hoylake described what was to become the site of the Royal Liverpool Golf Club as 'very sandy, very bare of trees, and smelling strongly of shrimps'.

The Tower Theatre, New Brighton.

One major Wallasey Theatre that has survived into the twenty-first century is the Irving Theatre, albeit as a bingo hall. Built in 1899 and opened by Sir Henry Irving himself on the understanding that only high-quality plays would be performed there, the opening performance involved no fewer than sixty performers. Irving's high-quality diktat was soon forgotten, however, and musical comedies of varying standard became the norm. As with most theatres, The Irving embraced the new demand for moving pictures and began showing short films of royal visits and other local events. From 1908 performances became dependant on the seasons, films being shown in summer and plays in winter. Live performances ended in 1936 and films ended in March 1959 with a showing of *Sea of Sand* starring Dickie Attenborough, after which it became a bingo hall, which it remains.

Several more purpose-built theatres opened up in New Brighton before the First World War, challenging the pre-eminence of the Tower. The first of these to arrive was the Winter Gardens in Alexandra Road, handily positioned near to New Brighton railway station. Formerly known as the Alexandra Hall, this incarnation failed after just one year. One reason may be deduced from the first act to appear. The Horbury Hand Bell Ringers probably did their best, but it does not really sound like much of a gig. The name was quickly changed to The Winter Gardens in 1908 with a mixture of plays, variety shows and silent film presentations. Opera appeared later with the D'Oyly Carte troupe performing *Gilbert and Sullivan* to packed audiences. Rebuilt in 1931, the building was sold to the Cheshire Picture Halls company, which converted it into a cinema with occasional plays. Yet again the irresistible siren call of bingo brought tombola to the Winter Gardens in

The Irving Theatre, Borough Road, Seacombe.

The Tivoli Theatre from the beach, New Brighton.

1965, with the building surviving until 1991. A greater threat to the Tower Theatre was the Tivoli, which opened up literally in the shadow of the tower in Easter 1914. Variety shows, repertory and local operatics were the order of the day with such luminaries as Tommy Handley, Gracie Fields and Anne Heywood treading the boards. Advertised as 'Wirrals Own Theatre' the thousand-seater auditorium proved to be a most popular venue for local people. Its distinctive architecture is well-remembered by many older residents with its dome and twin pyramids at the front of the building facing onto Tower Promenade. There was a small arcade of shops below Reeces cafeteria on the balcony, these included Gordons Ice Cream Parlour and Arthur Moss's souvenir shop. The main entrance was between these shops and led into the stalls, downstairs bar and the boxes. Bombed in the Second World War, it reopened in May 1945 with an appearance by Nosmo King. All was swept away in 1976 after a short life as a rather tawdry amusement arcade.

The final theatre of the trio was the most successful of them all. What everyone in Wirral knows as the Floral Pavilion started life as the Victoria Pavilion, which was opened in May 1913 as an open-air summer theatre. Built on land made available by the demolition of the infamous Ham and Egg Parade, it specialised in variety shows and other low-brow entertainment, which drew in the day trippers by the thousand. It was enlarged in 1925 into a 1,200-seat theatre and given a much-needed iron and glass roof. Notable entertainers from the time included Rob Wilton and Tommy Handley, followed latterly by Dickie Henderson. In 1948 Jackson Earles Melody Inn Revue made its first appearance, which continued every year until the early 1970s. The theatre was rebuilt in 1965 and reopened as the Floral Pavilion. This incarnation was fairly short-lived and

The Floral Pavilion, New Brighton.

was demolished in 2006. The new Floral Pavilion was finished in 2008 at a cost of £12 million. Ken Dodd played the final night in the old theatre and the first night in the new. It is rumoured that he had remained on stage during this time and they had built the new Floral around him.

One more theatrical establishment deserves an honourable mention here, namely the Little Theatre in Grange Road West in Birkenhead. Local repertory company the Carlton Players had been looking for a suitable permanent home and a former Presbyterian church in the town seemed to fit the bill, although the task of converting it from a place of worship to a place of entertainment was quite a daunting task. The entire troupe mucked in and luckily many were tradesmen who offered their expertise for the common good and for minimal cost managed to convert the basement into a foyer and separate rehearsal and dressing rooms. It is a most interesting building to visit for a night's entertainment as many of the church features have been retained and it still has the appearance of a religious building. The Carlton Players put on six different plays throughout the season from slapstick farces to serious drama. The Floral Pavilion, the Little Theatre and the Gladstone Theatre in Port Sunlight are the main venues for drama on Wirral.

The earliest purpose-built cinemas as opposed to other premises converted into picture houses were the Liscard Palace and The Queens Picture House, both opening in Wallasey in 1911 and both buildings surviving into the twenty-first century. The Queens was the first by just three weeks, opening in Poulton Road on 4 November 1911 with a range of films

The Little Theatre, Grange Road West, Birkenhead.

including drama, comedy and news. The building boasted a curved glass veranda to keep the patrons dry in inclement weather, an impressive dome above, and a plastered exterior that was enhanced at night by 350 electric light bulbs. The interior was equally grandiose with a lushly carpeted marble entrance and crimson plush upholstery. The gradual decline in customers forced the Queens closure in July 1959 and the building, stripped of its finery, became a car showroom and then a supermarket, to which it remains.

The Liscard Electric Palace opened on 25 November 1911 and became one of Wallasey's most popular venues. The white plastered frontage was a sight to behold, with cartouches, swags and ornament aplenty, the symmetry completed with two large Diocletian windows. As with the Queens, all this was lit up at night. Once inside the patrons approached a foyer up a small flight of stairs and across a marble floor to a bow-shaped kiosk and a spiral staircase to the balcony. The eventual decline was assuaged by the introduction of cinemascope in 1955, but this fine cinema succumbed to the inevitable in 1959. Shorn of its beautiful if gaudy ornamentation, the building still stands in Seaview Road and is currently a shoe shop.

The former Queens
Picture House, Poulton
Road, Wallasey.

The former Liscard Palace, Seaview Road, Wallasey.

The most popular cinema in Wallasey was The Capitol, due to a large extent to its central location in Liscard. The designers took full advantage of the prime site, covering the building with glazed white terracotta and a large glass veranda. Fourteen shops were also included in the scheme. Opened on 4 September 1926 by the lord mayor, all proceeds from the first night were donated to nearby Victoria Central Hospital. Closed in 1959 for a total regeneration and renamed The ABC, the cinema never fully regained the following it had before the closure despite the many improvements. As part of the ABC cinema group regular Saturday matinees were held with a mixture of films, serials such as Batman, and live performances by local children who were brave enough or daft enough to get up on stage and perform to an audience of raucous kids. Talented children managed to leave the stage unscathed, but those whose performance was deemed under par were pelted with whatever the baying mob had to hand; on one occasion a couple of carrots were thrown at a particularly inept accordion player, whether these vegetables had been brought into the cinema for that express purpose is unclear. With falling attendances, the upstairs café was opened as a club with performances by various bands, including Thin Lizzy before they found fame with a wider audience. The ABC closed in 1974 but many of the shops have found alternative uses. One other cinema building survives in Wallasey, albeit as a snooker club. The Royal in King Street Egremont was opened in 1912 and was the very first cinema in the area to have a stereophonic sound system. It closed in 1967 with a double bill of *Day of the Triffids* and *King Kong v. Godzilla*.

Back in Birkenhead a host of purpose-built cinemas were built between 1911 and 1920. The Electric Picture Palace was the first, built on the site of a former chapel, opening in November 1911 to the strains of the Delmont Orchestra (no soundtracks then). Although it was a small cinema, it proved very popular with the good people of Rock Ferry, 'Take your Alice to The Palace' was the advice given out by the publicity department. It later became THE place for westerns and it was a sad day in the area when it closed in 1959 and was converted for Palace Motors. Another Rock Ferry cinema was The Lyceum in New Chester Road, which showed silent films intermingled with slide shows with news from the First World War, accompanied by the strains of the French national anthem by the full resident orchestra. A name change to The Essoldo did not alter its fate, however, and it closed in 1962, becoming a supermarket.

DID YOU KNOW?
At the corner of the huge Ritz Cinema in Birkenhead a circular tower of steel and glass rose 70 feet from the ground and was well illuminated at night. During the Second World War the lights were extinguished and a powerful air-raid siren was set up inside, which could be heard over a mile away.

The ABC Capitol Cinema, Liscard, *c.* 1960.

Staff outside the Palace Picture House at Rock Ferry.

Auditorium to the Ritz Cinema, Birkenhead.

Birkenhead went large after 1930 when the arrival of talking pictures massively increased the popularity of the cinema, making it the most popular pastime in Britain. Huge cinemas were constructed with seating capacities ranging from 1,300 to an incredible 2,500. The Avenue Picture House, opened by the mayor and closed by the Germans, seated 1,200. The Rialto and The Regal, both in Bebington, boasted a similar number. The Plaza had room for 2,500 patrons and the Gaumont, which still stands in Park Road East, accommodated 1,700. The main façade of the latter has changed little and still has three round sculptures featuring a pierrot, a pierrette and a clown. It housed a skating rink in the 1990s for a short while and is now a furniture warehouse. The apogee in cinema construction, however, was the enormous 2,500-seat Ritz in Claughton Road. Considered the finest cinema outside the West End, it was dubbed 'the Showplace of the North'. This white Portland stone colossus covered an area of over an acre and was officially opened in 1938 by Gracie Fields who sang 'Sally' (did she know any other songs?) to a rapturous crowd estimated to be over 75,000, which included the mayors of Birkenhead, Wallasey, Bebington and Liverpool. The opening night continued with a *Popeye* cartoon, Reginald Foort and his Grand Organ, the famous Dagenham Girl Pipers, and Steffani and his Singing Songsters. Late in the evening they finally got around to showing a film. Many smaller cinemas had opened in Wirral such as The Kings in Heswall and The Tudor in West Kirby, both of which survive in different guises. None of these however came anywhere near matching the picture palaces of the bigger towns.

The Halfway House and proposed cinema site, Prenton.

There were a few cinemas that never left the drawing board, including a 1,200 seater proposed for a site on the junction of Teehey Lane and Village Road in Bebington where the Acorn pub now stands. No name was ever suggested for this cinema but one that nearly came to fruition was the Curzon, this was to be sited next to the Half-Way House in Prenton and foundations were actually laid, but the Second World War scuppered these plans and the cinema was never built. The Regal cinema was planned for a site in Wallasey Road near to the old market and another in Bromborough near to The Cross. At least Bromborough did eventually get their cinema but they had to wait nearly forty years.

The heyday of the cinema was in 1946 with 1,640 million visits being recorded. This staggering total had declined to a mere 70 million by 1976, with the usual reason being the increase in television ownership. This was not the whole story, however, as high entertainment taxes and rates also played a part. One further factor not always realised was the fact that a lot of the films were not very good. The American studios continued to make good feature films but there was a noticeable decline in the standard of British films, notwithstanding Hammer Horror, James Bond and the earlier Carry On films. The industry reached its nadir in the 1970s with a series of dire comedies and TV spin-offs.

Alternative pastimes have always been readily available to the people of Wirral. Surrounded as it is by the sea, swimming and sailing have always been popular. Naked and semi-naked sea bathing was the norm before the advent of public swimming pools, frequently outraging public decency according to newspaper reports of the time. Partly to allay public concerns, the peninsula became home to a large number of bathing pools, most of which were outdoor and ranged from the intimate dimensions of Parkgate and Port Sunlight baths to the largest in the world at the time at New Brighton. The earliest was constructed in stages from 1913 after pressure from the recently formed West Kirby Swimming Club, which had utilised the large marine lake up to this point. A large

The former Tudor Cinema in West Kirby.

Hoylake Baths, *c.* 1935, with poseur (top left).

concrete shelter was provided on the landward side with concrete curtains reaching out into the lake. The western edge remained open to the open water, however, which was unfortunate in the jellyfish season when the lifeguards had to scoop them out with nets before they reached the bathers. A floating diving platform was provided in 1920 and after a refurbishment in 1930 a concrete island was created that housed diving boards and a water chute. Just along the coast a similar pool was created at Hoylake in 1913 and this was also upgraded in the 1920s with additional facilities.

Lord Leverhulme had been ahead of the curve as usual, however, as he had provided his staff with an oval-shaped swimming pool in Port Sunlight village way back in 1902. The public were allowed to use the facilities but Levers workers benefited from dedicated sessions for an entrance fee of 1*d.* Built by one of Lever's preferred architectural practices, William and Segar Owen, the pool was 100 feet long and contained 225,000 gallons of water, which was filtered and heated to 60 degrees before being pumped from the Port Sunlight Works nearby. One of the quirkier facilities was the dressing huts at the side of the pool, which were thatched. It was unfortunately demolished in 1975 and a garden centre eventually took the site.

Another small privately funded pool was created on the front at Parkgate in 1923 by A. G. Grenfell, then headmaster at the nearby Mostyn House School. Originally built for the exclusive use of pupils from the school, it soon became available for the general public to enjoy and became very popular, especially when a children's pool was added in 1930. The fact that the water was sourced from the River Dee became a serious problem when the estuary became increasingly clogged with silt and spartina grass, which had been introduced on the Welsh side of the Dee to stabilise the shifting channels. Closed in 1942, it reopened briefly from 1947 but closed permanently in 1950. It is now a car park for Wirral Country Park.

Port Sunlight Baths from a Lever Brothers postcard.

Parkgate Baths in the 1930s.

OPEN AIR BATHS. NEW FERRY.   No 4.

New Ferry Baths around 1935.

Many locals fondly remember New Ferry Baths, which opened in 1932 at a cost of £12,000. It was a rather featureless affair with large grassed areas to the sides and a small shelter at one end. At 330 feet long and 90 feet wide, it used 1 million gallons of water drawn from the Mersey. While researching these baths it was noted that many patrons boasted of 'bunking in' for free but also mentioned that it was a shame that they had pulled it down. It seems not to have occurred to anyone that the baths may have stayed open longer if they had not been deprived of all that lost revenue. Perhaps the least well known of all Wirral's open-air baths, but one of the finest was Rivacre Baths near Ellesmere Port, which opened in 1934. The T-shaped pool had fountains, crazy paving and ornamental gardens where patrons could relax and sunbathe. A café and a children's playground was also provided. Closed in 1981, it was demolished in 1985 to make way for a small housing estate.

Wallasey had two open-air baths, with by far the smaller of the two being the Derby Pool at Harrison Drive. Opened by Lord Derby on 8 June 1932 at a cost of £50,000, it proved popular for many years despite the permanently freezing water, which was drawn from the Mersey nearby. On sunny summer days it was difficult to find a space to sunbathe or even to lay your towel because of the large crowds that flocked here. A restaurant now occupies part of the site. Opened two years later, New Brighton Baths dwarfed its neighbour. Built as part of a proposed scheme of art deco hotels and entertainment centres, which was to line Kings Parade all the way to Harrison Drive, the baths were the only part of the development to be built as the onset of the Second World War delayed and then ended these ambitious plans. The pool, however, was at the time of construction the largest such facilities in the world, covering 4.5 acres at a cost of £103,000. The pool was officially opened by Lord Leverhulme on the 13 June 1934, attended by 12,000 invited guests, and proved immensely popular from the start. 100,000 people attended by the end of the first week, with the 1 million mark being reached within four months. The south-facing design took advantage of the maximum amount of sunlight and included a restaurant, four shops and a cavernous changing area which reached around the north-west corner in a great crescent, lit by glasscrete panels, which let the light flood in. Unfortunately, the panels between the changing booths were made of asbestos, the dangers of which were clearly not known at the time. There was a freezing stretch of water that bathers had to negotiate before getting to the pool, which was soaked in disinfectant, so at least if you contracted asbestosis you would be spared the added anguish of a verruca. Once in the water, patrons could use the three slides at the water's edge or sit in the large fountain, which was actually part of the filtration system for the pool. The more daring swimmer could test their mettle in the diving area which provided diving boards at various heights, from the lower spring board (the bottom springy) to the higher fixed boards, then another spring board (the top springy) culminating in the highest boards which were ten metres above the water and certainly not for the faint hearted. Whilst it was invigorating

ENTRANCE TO THE NEW BRIGHTON SUPER BATHING POOL. W.S.32.

New Brighton Baths entrance façade, c. 1936.

but slightly dangerous to hurl your scrawny carcass off the top board, the real peril was in lingering in the fifteen foot deep landing area too long, as it was ever-likely that the next plunging Herbert could well land on your head. The statistics for the pool were all impressive, room for 4,000 bathers and 20,000 spectators, 2,000 dressing lockers, and a capacity of 1.4 million gallons of water which could be emptied in eight hours which it was regularly done when the popular Miss New Brighton pageant was in town. Started in 1949, it continued until 1989 with Anne Heywood the famous actress winning the event in 1950. One other major event took place in 1984 when the New Brighton Rock event took place at the baths. Frankie Goes to Hollywood, Spandau Ballet, Madness and Nik Kershaw were just some of the stars on the bill. It is worth speculating whether the baths would still be here if they had not been undermined during the terrible storms that hit the coast in February 1990.

When sports are mentioned in relation to Wirral, the first thing most people would probably mention is golf by reason of The Royal Liverpool Golf Club which has played host to the British Open Golf Tournament on many occasions. This was not however the first sport played on the hallowed turf at Hoylake. Horse racing had been established here from 1830, in part to attract visitors to the area of 'the right sort', not the hoi polloi who were being attracted to nearby New Brighton. Horses were raced over an open course in the formative years before the area was railed off in the 1840's into a pear-shaped course. Exclusivity was the order of the day with entrants limited to members of the Royal Hunt Club. This was to prove problematic, partly as the course was very difficult to reach at the time, and the parochial qualification policy meant that far few horses were eligible to race. The attendance at meetings picked up however when the entry rules were relaxed and steeplechases were introduced to the card. Hoylake station had also been built nearby, increasing the accessibility that was not entirely welcomed by the Hunt Club members. As a way of raising additional revenue part of the course was sold off to a small cadre of Scottish golf enthusiasts who created a nine- hole golf course to the south-west of the racecourse. With the decline in interest for horse racing and a rapid increase in interest for golf, the former ended in around 1892 and the golf course expanded into the world famous eighteen holes we have today.

Considering there are no racecourses on Wirral today, it is perhaps surprising to learn that there have been no fewer than eleven based on the peninsula over the years. Most have been very short lived such as those at Hooton Park in the grounds of Hooton Hall, Poulton at the bottom of Gorsey Lane, Upton near to the Manor, Bidston near to the station, Rock Ferry by the Derby Arms, a very small one in Oxton and one at the top of Storeton Hill. A hunting lodge at the top of Storeton Hill was used as a grandstand to watch steeplechases in the fields below and this structure still survives. More notable was the course in Neston, on Windle Hill to the north of Hinderton Hall which existed between 1728 and 1846. Its main claim to fame was the appearance of a horse called 'Sir William' who won a race here and went on to win the Grand National at Aintree, the only horse ever to win a race on Wirral and the National. The course at Leasowe is probably the one most people will be aware of and was used from the 1500s onwards. Despite a popular belief, nearby Leasowe Castle was not constructed as a stand to watch the races, it was clearly defensive because of its massive construction, which would have been

New Brighton Baths in 1936.

New Brighton Baths in the 1960s.

THE ROYAL LIVERPOOL GOLF CLUB, HOYLAKE

Royal Liverpool Golf Club, Hoylake.

totally unnecessary and expensive for a mere grandstand. It was an open course of some 5 miles stretching from Wallasey Village to the castle and back with stabling in Jockey Lane (now Sandcliffe Road). It was not lack of support which eventually closed Wallasey racecourse but the gradual encroachment of the Irish Sea. One of the most popular races known as the Wallasey Stakes was moved to Newmarket and is reputed to have mutated into The Derby. As at Hoylake the increasing interest in golf, especially links courses, led to the land being sold to Leasowe and Wallasey Golf Clubs who utilised it to form two fine courses.

The rise in interest in golf on Wirral was mainly due to a large increase in Scottish immigrants moving to Liverpool who soon eyed up the potential in the vast tracts of sandhills across the Mersey. This land provided endless opportunities for the creation of golf links, the most famous being The Royal Liverpool Golf Club noted above, the royal element referring to the patronage of The Duke of Connaught, seventh child and third son of Queen Victoria. The course was laid out by Robert Chambers and George Morris who was the younger brother of the famous golfer Tom Morris, winner of the British Open on no fewer than four occasions in the 1860's, all at Prestwick. The Club has a string of firsts to its name, including holding the first amateur championships in 1885, the first international match in 1902 between England and Scotland, and the first transatlantic tournament between Great Britain and the USA in 1921, which went on to become the Walker Cup and returned to Hoylake in 2019. It has held the Open on twelve occasions. Winners include such legends as Bobby Jones, Walter Hagen and Tiger Woods. The Women's Open was held here in 2012. Another links course worthy of note is Wallasey

Leasowe Castle.

Golf Club, which was laid out by Tom Morris himself in 1891 and has held qualifying rounds for the Open in 1930, 1936 and 1956 when a youthful Gary Player participated. A greater claim to fame for the cub is its association with Dr Frank Stableford who invented the eponymous set of rules known and played worldwide.

One final course deserving of mention is the Wirral Ladies Golf Club in Bidston, the oldest such club in Britain and the only one wholly owned and run by women in Europe. Founded in 1894 by Herbert Potter, a member of the Royal Liverpool Golf Club, for the use of golfers wives and their friends, it was laid out as a nine hole course on 50 acres of Oxton Common. Male help was needed to get the club underway as it was very difficult for women to sign contracts at the time. Potters motives may appear a bit suspect as it was said that he only did it to keep women out of his own club, but whatever his reasons, his wife became the first club captain and it went from strength to strength, expanding into an eighteen-hole course in 1928 when land was purchased from the Earl of Shrewsbury for 1s per acre.

Wirral had at one time two clubs in the Football League: New Brighton and Tranmere Rovers, with the latter being the most successful. Founded in 1884, its history has been well documented. Two lesser-known facts may be appropriate here however and both relate to the stands at their Prenton Park ground. The stand known as the Cowshed is not merely a nickname because of its general appearance, part of the original structure actually came from a farm. A little-known fact about the Kop is that when the banking of the stand required raising, ten hundredweight tank traps left over from the Second World

Wallasey Golf Club.

Wirral Ladies Golf Club.

War were brought into service to increase the height. New Brighton FC only lasted from 1923 until 1951 when they were unceremoniously booted out of the league because of their poor attendances, averaging just 4,000 patrons per game. Many more leisure pursuits and sports are enjoyed on Wirral but space precludes a discussion on all of them. Cricket, tennis, rugby, bowls, and water sports are all very popular, cycling and walking in Wirral is always rewarding. Whichever activity you choose, however, it could not be undertaken in more attractive surroundings than on the beautiful peninsula of Wirral.

TRANMERE ROVERS F.C.
CHAMPIONS DIV. III (N.), 1937–38

Tranmere Rovers football team in the 1937/38 season.